P9-APO-377

$4.00

Simulation Gaming for Management Development

Simulation Gaming for Management Development

JAMES L. MCKENNEY
Associate Professor of Business Administration
Harvard University

DIVISION OF RESEARCH
GRADUATE SCHOOL OF BUSINESS ADMINISTRATION
HARVARD UNIVERSITY
BOSTON · 1967

© Copyright 1967
By the President and Fellows of Harvard College

228973

Library of Congress Catalog Card No. 67–23304

PRINTED IN THE UNITED STATES OF AMERICA

ABSTRACT

Simulation Gaming for Management Development

This book reports the results of a research project which from the beginning has had dual objectives. One objective has been to develop an effective simulation model which would be suitable for a management game. The second objective has been pedagogical in character: "How can such a simulation model be used in gaming to contribute effectively to the development of business managers?"

Gaming as an educational device is not new; it has been employed in military training for many years. On the other hand, computer simulation is relatively novel, and the combination of computer simulation models and the gaming format for management training is still in its infancy. This study reports and analyzes the experience with gaming at the Harvard Business School as well as the character and results of the experimentation with gaming.

James L. McKenney, the author, is Associate Professor of Business Administration at the Harvard Business School and Associate Director for Research in the Data Processing Bureau.

This monograph describes the philosophy and structure of the present Harvard Business School Management Simulation Game. As such, it is a description of the product and process of eight years of research and development on the use of simulation gaming in an MBA curriculum. The purpose of this description is to provide an individual concerned with management development a basis for considering the use of such a simulation in training business administrators. In the introduction, the monograph discusses the evolution of war gaming as a basis for present business gaming and then describes the evolution of the present simulation model. The intent of this description is to provide an insight into simulation gaming in general, and in particular how the present simulation game was developed. The remainder of the volume is a detailed description of the output of the simulation model and how it has been utilized in a variety of business games. The study was undertaken not only to provide background for the consideration of the pros and cons of using a game, but also as a reference to enable the teacher-administrator to develop his own simulation game with the model.

One of the prime teaching objectives in this development effort has been the integration of various functional courses of Marketing, Production, and Finance, into an overall strategy implementation exercise. In addition, the game is intended to involve the participants in the utilization of analytical techniques in a dynamic problem-solving activity. Finally, it was developed to require a group of individuals to cooperate and communicate over a period of time toward the joint solution of a very complex problem.

Operationally, the simulation game has been designed to accomplish these goals over an elapsed period of time. This period includes adequate time for the introduction and three hours of student involvement for each move. The accomplishment of the present objectives seemed to take at least eight to twelve moves. The simulation was developed to allow an administrator to utilize the simulation model without any programming expertise or without any specific knowledge of how the particular model functions. In essence it is a black box which an individual might use as he would a case, a book, or a prepared lecture to accomplish teaching objectives as the individual sees fit in a given curriculum.

In general, the simulation model has been developed to be used in a teaching environment in groups of 20 or more students. The students are grouped into sets of four- or five-man entities called "firms." Each firm competes in an industry with from four to nine other firms. The industry is an economic abstraction of a consumer goods market programmed to be simulated on an electronic digital computer. Each firm competes in this industry by preparing a set of decisions on budgets which are transformed into appropriate inputs to the simulation model. The model is then run to produce a set of accounting statements providing data on which the participants make analyses for the next set of moves. The budgets the firms must prepare are on variables such as amount of labor per product or amount of advertising per quarter for each simulated decision period. At the start of the simulation the firms are given a history of their firm activities for the prior year. The model has been developed to require about ten to twelve hours of individual analysis per move. We have found allowing only three hours of elapsed time forces the students to organize and divide the job into parts which must be coordinated. In addition, the simulation includes long-run implications as well as short-run reactions for each decision. Thus the group must organize itself to accomplish a task which has short-run and long-run implications and in brief presents a realistic business-like problem.

A necessary role to make a simulation game a meaningful learning experience is the counseling and guidance from the Faculty. Our Faculty operate most successfully as a Board of Directors for each firm. The directors' purpose is to raise meaningful questions, give appropriate assignments, and probe the students to consider why they are making their decisions. The role of the Faculty is discussed in great detail throughout the present monograph.

This particular simulation game has been used as a required course in the first year of the MBA Program to accomplish the defined goals above. It has also been used in an Advanced Management Program as an exercise in strategy implementation as an adjunct to the Business Policy course. Finally, it has been used in a short course of two weeks as a main educational experience for a firm's management.

(Published by Division of Research, Harvard Business School, Soldiers Field, Boston, Mass. 02163. xvi + 189 pp. $4.00 1967.)

HD
29
.9
M3

Foreword

This monograph reports the results of a research project of several years' duration which from the beginning has had dual objectives. One objective has been to develop an effective simulation model which would be suitable for a management game. Such a model was to be sufficiently complex to challenge and motivate graduate students in business administration, yet manageable and economical in use. The monograph describes the current form of this simulation model and its evaluation in detail.

The second objective of the research was pedagogical in character. How can such a simulation model be used in gaming to contribute effectively to the development of business managers? The experience with gaming at the Harvard Business School, and the character and results of the experimentation with gaming here are also reported and analyzed.

Gaming as an educational device is not new. It has been employed in military training for many years. On the other hand, computer simulation is relatively novel, and the combination of computer simulation models and the gaming format for management training is still in its infancy. Because many schools and business organizations are beginning to use such management games, and because this particular game was designed to be exportable for the use of others, this account of the Harvard Business School management game, the process of its development, and its use is being published in this partial form. The model itself, of course, cannot be published in book form; it is available only as a deck of punched cards or a magnetic tape. It too, however, is available for any potential user of the game.

This somewhat unusual type of research venture at the School was financed primarily by the income of an endowment fund for research which came from an anonymous donor. The International

Business Machines Corporation also provided partial support by contributing funds for Professor McKenney's one-year appointment as an IBM Fellow at the Harvard Computing Center. We are indebted to both of these donors for the support of this research.

BERTRAND FOX
Director of Research

Soldiers Field
Boston, Massachusetts
June 1967

Preface

This is a description of the process and product of the development of a management simulation game. The function of the *process* is to tailor a simulation model and to develop a game that will complement and contribute to the teaching objectives of a given curriculum. An important *product* of this process is the establishment of a tradition of gaming in the environment. A vital element of this tradition is a commitment to continual appraisal and improvement of the gaming effort. This account is provided to allow interested individuals, who are considering the introduction of gaming, not only to appreciate the product, but to have a better understanding of the process.

It is hoped this volume will accelerate the effort of infusing the potential of gaming into the training of professional managers. Gaming can be a vital laboratory wherein we not only develop future managers, but investigate how future managers should function. We feel we are now entering this teaching and research stage which was the goal of our developmental effort. A recurring theme is that to attain meaningful success careful planning must precede a game in order to integrate and control a complex simulation game in coordination with the rest of the curriculum.

The data and experience related in this monograph are drawn from a diary on gaming, compiled since 1957. This diary summarizes a few of the significant developmental stages that influence present gaming and a few misconceptions of early gamesters. It focuses on the unique aspects of our efforts to create a meaningful experience for 670 graduate students in an economical fashion. Thus, it is a report on how to implement the folklore of gaming to take advantage of economies of scale and yet maintain the flavor of counseled competition.

The existence of this simulation game and its contribution to better management development are due in large part to the support of Associate Deans Hassler and Lombard of the Harvard Business School. Dean Hassler encouraged the author to begin the experiment as the basis for a better understanding of how such a game might be integrated into the Harvard Business School curriculum. Upon Dean Hassler's resignation, Dean Lombard continued the experiment and has been a constant source of support in obtaining resources and Faculty interest in the simulation game effort. His counsel and leadership not only gained acceptance of the game in the curriculum but have made significant improvements in the exercise as a learning experience. Throughout this experiment, Professor A. R. Dooley, formerly Area Chairman of Production, has always encouraged and backed the gaming efforts of the author.

This report of the development of simulation gaming is, in essence, an account of team effort involving the cooperation and commitment of a heterogeneous group of individuals dedicated to a common cause. Effective development of simulation games requires simulation designers, game administrators, faculty advisors, and active participants. In addition to the combined effort of several individuals who provided the essential variety of different backgrounds and perspectives, there was a high degree of involvement and intense individual motivation provided by the students.

Several designers have contributed to the present model, starting with the initiators at UCLA, modelers at other institutions, and colleagues on the Harvard Business School Faculty. In connection with this study, the entire process of gaming was stimulated by Professor James R. Jackson at UCLA, creator of the first business game for an MBA Program. He introduced me to the gaming business in 1957, and since that time he has been a source of positive suggestions on how to improve the process. The present success of the Harvard Business School game is due in no small part to Professor Jackson's genius and teaching capacity. A second source of creative suggestions as to how to make a simulation game a more stimulating and vital learning experience has been Dr. William R. Dill, formerly of Carnegie Institute of Technology and now at IBM. His efforts have made this game and gaming in general more relevant for professional business students. In addition, he has been a staunch partner in the investigation of how to improve the learning process through research on gaming activities. Professor Martin Shubik of Yale has significantly aided this effort by advancing the conceptual development of simulation modeling. Professor Shubik, at times provocative, but always informed, has made suggestions on how to improve the competitive environment and how to implement shrewder methods of modeling. He has aided the acceptance of the present simulation as a rich environment for graduate students.

The main reason for the existence of this simulation exercise has been the continuous participation and constructive criticism of my colleagues on the Harvard Business School Faculty. Professor A. N. Turner and I began the first simulation experiment in order to couple our courses, in the spring of 1961. The following year a committee was formed, including Professors Turner, C. J. Christenson, R. G. Brown (now of Stanford), R. D. Buzzell, E. A. Helfert, and J. L. McKenney, to experiment with two sections on the use of gaming. This was followed by another committee the following year of Professors J. H. McArthur, S. I. Buchin, G. W. Dalton, T. C. Raymond, and J. L. McKenney to design a simulation game for the entire first year of the Harvard Business School MBA curriculum. This committee spent long hours in developing an appropriate set of teaching objectives, how these objectives might be implemented, and the resultant changes in the model and the curriculum. In addition, these individuals were most effective as informed simulation gamesters who introduced the potential of gaming to the remainder of the Faculty.

Special mention should be made of Professor McArthur's interest and zeal in creating a viable finance section for the present model. Professor Stanley Buchin was a main source for the present accounting format and better definitions of terms as they related to the curriculum. Professor Donald Cox of the Marketing area contributed the design for Marketing Research and was instrumental in revising parts of the instructions. Of late, my colleague and recent committee participant has been Professor Warren McFarlan, who has taken the leadership in developing the simulation as a larger, more encompassing, simulation game exercise in the first year. He, with the cooperation of Professor John Seiler, has developed the model and the gaming exercise into a new era of gaming which actively involves the organizational behavior course in all aspects of controlling a diverse corporate structure. They are continuing the development of this particular simulation model in the HBS–MBA curriculum.

The various administrative roles have been superbly executed by a stalwart, unheralded set of individuals. First and foremost of these is Mrs. Patricia Glavin Colton who patiently developed, tested, and executed the administrative details for the bulk of the games reported. Mrs. Colton invented and performed the logistics of how to operate a simulation game with 670 students in 128 firms and 21 corporations. Her graciousness and capacity to deal with continual minor discontinuities made this particular simulation game usable.

A second significant contributor was Mr. Eldon Ziegler, who imaginatively programmed the present simulation model in a modular fashion so that it could be tinkered with continuously, yet in as undisruptable a fashion as possible. Two individuals, who were vital to the success of the operation, Mr. Robert Burns, Manager of Operations in the Harvard Computing Center, and Mr. Joseph Leuko, Supervisor of Operations, have expeditiously processed the simulation runs at the Harvard University Computer Center with as short as 20-minute turn-around time when needed. This operation has been particularly fortunate in having the services of Mrs. Anna Stefanakis and Mrs. Louise Sullivan, who time and time again accurately key punched 1280 cards in a brief span of time at odd hours.

A special note of thanks is due Professor Gordon Marshall and his WAC group who spent endless hours on the thankless task of trying to develop a set of instructions that would not overwhelm the student yet would allow the individual participant enough confidence to operate in the simulated environment. Owing to Professor Marshall's patient guidance, the current instructions have been revised no less than seven times to their present understandable state.

Seventy-nine members of the Harvard Business School Faculty have served as counselors in the role of Board of Directors to guide the participants in making the game a learning experience. Their imaginative approach to their roles as counselors have made this simulation game a meaningful aspect of the curriculum. In no small part the total success of the effort is the direct result of their constructive and thoughtful comments on how the game might be improved and how the experience may be made more meaningful to the HBS students.

Most of all, I am indebted to the thousands of students who participated as managers of firms and demonstrated the learning potential of simulation gaming. Their enthusiastic response and, in the main, thoughtful approach stimulated a continual effort to improve the learning experience and make their investment of time worthwhile.

I am also most grateful to Miss Constance Lussier, my secretary, who not only wrote endless memoranda and revisions of the instructions but patiently served as general handyman in assisting people running games, dealing with the logistics of computers, spending odd hours of the day and night coping with student problems, and typing endless drafts of this monograph.

Many thanks are offered to the individuals who helped bring this particular piece of writing into being. First, there are the patient ladies in the Dictaphone Department: Mrs. Theresa Sparks, Mrs. June Kingsbury, and Miss Susan Helvitz; they listened to a monologue which developed slowly, copy by copy, to its present state. Miss Lussier patiently transformed these notes to the present publication. Second, I owe a great debt to Mrs. Nina Dolben and Miss Hilma Holton for their superb editorial comments which transformed my style into English. In addition, Professor E. P. Learned's enthusiasm and constructive suggestions aided immeasurably in orienting the meaning of these comments. Miss Holton made the development from manuscript to book most enjoyable.

The interest and spirit of this monograph are in existence and in better focus due primarily to the patient coaching and criticism of Professors Bertrand Fox and Richard Rosenbloom. Professor Fox's continuous support of an unusual research venture made it possible to develop the simulation to a usable state. The insight of Professor Rosenbloom's comments and queries on the nature of simulation gaming made the process more meaningful to me. Not only did these men encourage the development, but they reviewed the several drafts of the monograph to make it readable. The author will long remember Professor Fox's "k" next to awkward phrases and Professor Rosenbloom's two "question marks" over unclear paragraphs. Their continuous support made the transformation of a strong commitment into a printable document a rewarding experience.

A final note of gratitude is due my wife, Mary, for continuous cheerful understanding when the model broke down, or key punchers mangled students' results, or overzealous students created chaos in the classroom, or drafts seemed to be worse than better; she always managed to put my spirits in perspective, enabling me to finish the task.

As writing is an individual process, I am solely responsible for the contents of this book reflecting my interpretation of a simulated world.

JAMES L. MCKENNEY

Soldiers Field
Boston, Massachusetts
June 1967

CONTENTS

CHAPTER I Introduction to Business Gaming 1
Definition of a Management Simulation Game 2
The Why of Business Gaming 3
Guidelines to Good Gaming 7
The Heritage of War Gaming 7
Concluding Remarks 12

CHAPTER II The Evolution of the HBS Management Simulation Game 14
Development of the First Simulation Model 16
MBA Trial Runs 17
UCLA Simulation Game #2 18
First Uses of Model #2 19
Conclusions on Game #2 Experience 20
The Development of UCLA Model #3 21
Effective Uses of Model #3 25
Early Gaming in the HBS–MBA Program 25
1962 Simulation Developments 26
Conclusions Resulting from the 1962 Game Sessions 28
Development of the 1963 HBS Simulation Game 30
Conclusions Resulting from the 1963 Game Sessions 34
Tactical Problems of Game Design 35
Conclusions 36

CHAPTER III The Present Simulation Model 38
The Overall Design of the Simulation 39
The Spirit of the Marketing, Production, and Financial Aspects of the Model 43
The Structure of the Information 44
The Marketing Characteristics of the Simulation 50
Definition of the Influence of Demand Determinants . . 52

The Most Important Demand Determinant: Product Price 54
How the Product Quality Image Is Determined 55
Varying Time Impact of Marketing Budgets 56
Market Research 58
Competitive Aspects of the Model 59
The Production Aspects of the Simulation 62
Production Capacity 63
Indirect Costs and Labor Inefficiencies 64
Calculation of Production Output 66
The Finance Aspects 68
Cash Requirements 69
Sources of Available Funds 71
Faculty Aids in the Model 77
Concluding Remarks on the Model 80

CHAPTER IV Game Design 82
Faculty Game Activities 82
Guides to Game Development 85
Design Decisions in Developing a Complementary Game 86
Pre-Game Session Activities 87
Observations on Student Reaction: Folklore of Gaming . . 89
Course Game Assignments 92
Pertinent Game-Written Assignments 93
Conclusion 95

CHAPTER V Recent Gaming Experience 96
Description of the Spring 1965 HBS–MBA Management Game 96
The 1966 HBS Simulation Game 102
The Use of the HBS Simulation in an Advanced Management Program Session 105
A Company Program 108
Concluding Remarks 112

CHAPTER VI Gaming Research 114
Initial Game Experimentation at the Harvard Business School 115
The First Evaluation Experiment 115

The Second Evaluation Experiment 116
A "Need for Achievement" Trial 118
A Statistical Search As a Basis for Further Research 119
1965 Game Research at the Harvard Business School . . 120
Experimental Design 122
Learning Agenda and Their Effects 124
The Influence of Faculty Boards 124
Experienced versus Newly Formed Teams 126
Organizing Firms by Ability 127
Conclusion 131
Future Game Research 133

APPENDIX A: HBS Management Simulation Instructions to Participants 137
Table of Contents 140

APPENDIX B: Management Control Methods—The Cash Forecast 183

BIBLIOGRAPHY 187

List of Tables

I. Threshold Budgets of Market Research Expenditures . . 58
II. Implicit Expenses of a Firm 70
III. Communication of Intended Faculty Roles 125
IV. Normalized Profit and Sales Performance Against Ability Measures 128
V. Average Measures of Individual Attitudes and Perceptions Against Ability Level of Group 130

List of Exhibits

1. Management Simulation—Income Statement for a Typical Firm 40
2. Management Simulation—Decision Form 46
3. Industry Information on Competitors 48
4. Product Income Statement 60
5. Balance Sheet and Cash Flow 72

6. HBS Faculty Report of Each Firm in an Industry 78
7. 1965 HBS Management Simulation Schedule 97
8. 1966 HBS Management Simulation Schedule 104
9. Flow Diagram of Production Process 107

APPENDIX A
I. *Mangement Simulation—Decision Form* 158
II. *Income Statement* 160
III. *Balance Sheet* 164
IV. *Product Statement* 168
V. *Industry Report* 172
VI. *Standard Production Hours of Output Obtained from Each Man Each Week in a Quarter* 174
VII. *Work Sheet for Product X, Dept. Y* 176
VIII. *Production Delays and Inventories* 178
IX. *Relationship Between Size of Production Increase and Time to Implement Increase* 181
X. *Work Sheet (continued from Exhibit VII)* 182

Simulation Gaming for Management Development

CHAPTER I

Introduction to Business Gaming

This monograph is a description of the product and process of research on how to improve the managerial skills of MBA students by capitalizing on the involvement of simulation gaming. It is addressed to the teacher or administrator interested in utilizing a game in a program for training professional managers. To accommodate the potential range of interest in gaming, games in general are discussed, as well as the development, design, and method of implementation of the present game, and the research efforts employed to investigate gaming. Each topic is considered in a separate chapter to allow the reader to select topics in accordance with his interests. Thus, an individual considering gaming for the first time might obtain an overall view of the technique by reading the introductory chapter, the description of the present simulation model, and the elements of game design. An individual utilizing the Harvard Business School Management Game could obtain some perspective on its makeup by considering the developmental chapter and the detailed description which has proved useful as a reference for preparing an introduction to the rules. A game developer looking for new ideas might peruse the chapters on developmental efforts, on alternative methods of implementing games, and on research efforts.

A purpose of this discussion is to provide an understanding of the potential of business gaming for management development. Gaming is a pragmatic and nondirective approach in which the student is confronted with a businesslike problem which he must solve at his own pace. The game designer must develop integrated businesslike problems in such a manner that they will be challenging to the student over an extended period of time without overwhelming him at the start. Furthermore, these problems should provide insight into real-life decision-making activities and, where appropriate, be subject to discussion to enhance the learning potential of the exercise. The class of problems selected should allow the student to experiment with the concepts and attitudes he has been involved with in his course of study. Thus, the game developer has to structure data and simulation responses which stimulate the student to experiment with forming new habits of decision making, and he has to imbed this activity in a game environment which encourages reflection and discussion. In essence then, gaming is no different from other pedagogic approaches since it is an art of sequencing pertinent material which will induce intellectual growth and stimulate discussions to reinforce the learning process. It is a complex art because of the dynamic nature of the material.

Definition of a Management Simulation Game

Of the wide variety of business games in use, only that class referred to as general management simulation games will be considered. The word game in this discussion means a competitive mental activity wherein opponents compete through the development and implementation of an economic strategy. The three basic components of a simulation game are an abstraction of an economic environment, or a *model,* a series of rules for manipulation of the model, or *simulation,* and a set of rules which govern the activity of the participants in relation to the simulation, a *game*. The competitive activity is governed by the economic model which is a facsimile business environment whose basic design the participants cannot control. The participants do influence the economic development of the facsimile environment in the game by the implementation of their strategy. Essentially this economic model represents the demand function for an industry and the mechanism for determining the quantity of production given a schedule of resource allocation in the form of dollar budgets. The model itself is a series of equations representing a consumer market, a financial market, a productive capacity for each firm, and an accounting model which extracts cost and tabulates data for each firm. The word simulation refers to that portion of the activity wherein this economic abstraction is manipulated in accordance with a set of rules. An example of such a rule would be, "Select the minimum of inventoried material, allocated labor, and prior plant capacity as the production output for the decision period." The rules for manipulating the models considered are programmed for an IBM 7094 computer and include provision for creating a series of accounting statements on the state of the firm. The rules which govern the participants' relation with the simulated environment to create a game prescribe the number, form, and timing of a series of economic decisions for managing a facsimile firm.

The Why of Business Gaming

The prime appeal of gaming as a teaching tactic is that it generates a sustained, high level of student involvement. For management development this appeal is heightened by the opportunity to involve the student in a dynamic businesslike problem which the student must cope with over an extended period of time. This dynamic problem can and should include uncertain events, elements of risk, and a complex payoff function. The nature of the competitive game, if designed well, causes the student to identify with his role and to assume a responsible attitude toward his behavior and the game environment. He identifies the results of his move as a reflection on his business ability and typically devotes a sincere effort in the careful analysis of all available information to develop an appropriate set of future moves to improve his position. Game playing is an iterative process and, if the participant feels he can control the success of his firm in the game environment, he will accept the feedback information on how he has performed in the environment and will attempt to learn from his mistakes. Thus motivation, the opportunity to exercise analytical procedures in a complex environment, and prompt feedback are the prime reasons why the use of gaming has grown so dramatically in business curricula recently.

But why is it just a recent development? Certainly we have known of games for several years—centuries, in fact. Gaming in general involves participants; but involvement is not adequate for a training exercise. It must be meaningful involvement, and the participants must feel they are responsible for the outcome of their moves. Chance or cumbersome cause-effect relationships spoil the learning potential of game environments, and it was not until recently that a reasonable method for characterizing complex competitive situations was invented. Prior to the development of game theory, most games for training were war games with two opponents. These were quite elegant simulation games for developing operational expertise within the military. The simulations involved three-dimension maps, detailed replicas of forces, and large portfolios of background information to provide a data-rich environment in which challenging and complex military exercises could be conducted. There was no similar simulated data-rich environment available for the training of business managers, nor had there been much interest in codifying the competitive action of more than two but less than "n" opponents. It would seem, therefore, that until recently, in order to take advantage of the potential of gaming, adequate tools were lacking to develop an appropriate business game.

The vocabulary of game theory seems to have provided the final catalyst to allow sophisticated games to be developed in a variety of environments. Professor von Neumann demonstrated in the 1930s that all forms of competitive behavior, be it economic, military, or social, could be construed as a process of strategy development and implementation.[1] Such a strategy is defined by a series of decisions in an uncertain environment over an extended time horizon. The vocabulary of game theory provided a concise method of defining the characteristics of competition, such as number of competitors, form of competition, method of implementation, and the form of time horizons. In addition, game

[1] von Neumann and Morgenstern, *Theory of Games and Economic Behavior.*

N.B. SEE BIBLIOGRAPHY FOR COMPLETE REFERENCE INFORMATION.

theory provided a precise method for defining competitive moves in carrying out strategies.

Game theory research resulted in a series of elegant solutions for what would be trivial games in the real world. However, very complex games were defined and, although no solution was found, a good deal of insight was gained into how complex strategies could be described. Explicit definitions of complex games also delineated the decision-making process of competitors using a variety of strategies and how these strategies were modified because of new information. This effort of developing solutions and considering how responses might be made provided a background of experience on how to codify a set of interrelated moves of decisions in a competitive situation. The process of defining a set of possible actions or plans which were explicit descriptions of feasible strategies demonstrated the similarities between competition in economic and military environments.

During the period from 1946 to 1956 with the founding of the RAND Corporation and other civilian advisory groups, a concentrated effort was made to extend former war-gaming exercises into operational games for testing strategies for military operations. One environment for play was an abstraction of a military situation programmed for a computer to simulate how the environment might respond to a set of plans.[2] In addition, a few of these models allowed for human alteration of factors in the model to consider the effect of alternative estimates of response on a given plan. An outcome of these developments in operational gaming seems to have been the first business simulation game.[3] The innovators acknowledged the relationship to game theory and their recent experiences with operational gaming. Their description of the first simulation game was in game-theoretic terms although the authors were careful to point out that business games possess greater immediate usefulness than game theory for training decision makers.

The uniting of game experience with economic modeling skill might have been for naught had there not existed the computation capacity of the computer. This capacity has allowed the economic

[2] M. G. Weiner, *An Introduction to War Games,* p. 22.

[3] R. Bellman et al., "Construction of a Business Game," pp. 463–483.

model builders to create complex rules and yet avoid the drudgery of time-consuming calculations. In addition, the computer produces the results of moves of the participants in a printed form common to most business reports. The computation and printing capacity of the computer are a great help in creating the aura of verisimilitude and impartiality a convincing game requires without imposing the tiresome work and possible mistakes that a clerical process would involve.

The initial product of this operational gaming experience was, relative to other first new pedagogic attempts, a very sophisticated exercise. The first business simulation game involved five teams of managers, each of whom directed the economic activity of a facsimile firm that was competing in a simulated consumer market with other firms. The possible economic activity was defined by a group of operation researchers in an economic model which was programmed to be manipulated by an IBM 650 computer. The computer program generated automatically accountinglike reports for each firm to observe the results of its decisions. The accounting reports and the understandability of the original model allowed the authors to involve experienced businessmen in simulated techniques not heretofore possible.[4] The participants had the available information, felt they could control the operation of their firm, and were able to function in the simulated decision-making environment in a natural fashion.[5]

The computer's role in business gaming will not be discussed directly but it seems appropriate to emphasize the logistical support it provides. The computer not only reduces potential calculating errors, but it also eliminates the game administrator's detailed understanding of the model in order to conduct a game. Thus, with the black box of the computer program, with rules of how it operates, and what it purports to do without really being aware of the explicit design of the model and the rules for manipulating the abstraction, a teacher can conduct a gaming exercise. A final plus for computer calculation is that it is inexpensive. Models similar to the initial game require less than one dollar of computer time per participant for an entire game.

[4] *Ibid.*

[5] McDonald and Ricciardi, "The Business Decision Game," pp. 140–142.

Guidelines to Good Gaming

The art of modeling for business games has grown from the first game of five possible decisions to present games that require up to 300 decisions. However, three of the tenets that the early game designers espoused as crucial to success of the game are still quite pertinent.[6] These three guidelines of design are: (1) stability of the environment, (2) observable response to the decisions of the participants, and (3) no opportunity for the participant to use an unrealistic tactic to influence the outcome. The first concept or notion of stability means that the game should reward sound consistent playing. Thus, the model should react slowly in a realistic fashion and not respond to unusual actions but to actions in accordance with accepted business practice.

The second factor critical to the success of a game is elasticity, and it relates to the impact each decision has upon the total environment of the model. The rules for manipulating the model should produce some effect for every decision variable with the result that within a finite set of moves some environmental response can be observed. Finally, no gimmick should allow success. Since the purpose of the simulation game is training decision makers who are to operate in an uncertain environment, it is desirable to insure that the players act as they would in the actual business situation. Operation in the environment, then, means a careful analysis of the data and of the resulting synthesis of plans, not a careful analysis of the rules and data to manipulate winning. A teacher considering the use of a simulation should experiment with the model and its manipulation to insure that the model does not have any gimmicks, does respond to all the decisions, and encourages conscientious analysis and synthesis.

The Heritage of War Gaming

The above tenets relate to one component of the game, the simulated environment, and are based on the original designer's experience with operational gaming. As it is the purpose of this study to provide an overview of gaming and some background

[6] R. Bellman et al., "Construction of a Business Game," pp. 484–485.

for an appraisal of past gaming efforts, a broader perspective is needed. Military training through gaming has been going on for centuries and has developed from simple chess-like games in India in prehistoric times to today's month-long simulated worldwide games. Military gaming history beginning in the sixteenth century is particularly rich in anecdotes about the role of the instructor and typical student reaction and achievement.[7] This history is relevant for business gaming because the primary purpose of this gaming activity has been for the training of decision makers. A noted expert, General Rudolph Hoffman, a respected military leader in the German Army, sums up the general intent of war gaming in Germany prior to World War II: [8]

> The purpose of a war game is to train all ranks in estimating any given situation, the main emphasis being placed on a concise and logical presentation of ideas in making the resulting decisions as to how a combat objective is to be obtained and in issuing orders designed to achieve this objective.

General Hoffman noted that all members of the Army Officers Corps participated in several war games each year and that gaming was one of the most important activities in their officer training program.

War gaming, from its earliest inception to the present time, has involved two or more teams of participants competing against each other for control of an area in the game environment. Early games were primarily for developing an appreciation for possible military tactics utilizing military vocabulary.[9] They were conducted upon chess-like boards with men labeled to represent common military units. With the introduction of time as an element, in 1824 came the development of elaborate scale models used to teach implementation of tactics and to involve the students in a planning exercise.[10] Later, as politics and logistics both increased in importance for military games, extensive brochures were de-

[7] J. P. Young, *A Survey of War Games,* pp. 6–26.

[8] Rudolph Hoffman, "War Games," p. 2. He commanded the Eastern Front in World War II and assisted directing German war games for the general staff, starting in 1922.

[9] H. J. R. Murray, *A History of Board Games,* pp. 234–236.

[10] J. P. Young, "A Survey of War Games," p. 17.

veloped which defined the political setting of each combatant. These brochures defined the available resources in the simulated environment and provided a theme for the exercise with military goals for each side. The participants were expected to develop a strategy and supporting plans to accomplish their goals; for example, neutralization of a zone or integration of a country in an existing hegemony. By 1860 all the elements of modern gaming were involved: the notion of time, detailed simulation of activities, and cognizance of pertinent environmental forces.

War games were conducted by an umpire and a clerical staff, with the aid of a rule book. The rule book defined the elapsed time allowed for each move, how much simulated time the move represented, the steps to transform a decision into a series of simulated activities, and what decisions were to be made. The umpire decided what to do in unusual situations, including the outcome of most engagements, and he also was responsible for conducting a concluding session to review the decisions and activities of the participants.

Mathematical developments in military tactics in the early 1800s generated dissent against the arbitrariness of umpires and the vagueness of logistical information. As a result of this criticism, elaborate war game rules were devised for a sophisticated analysis of situations. Now a new dissent arose: critics labeled the models as too theoretical. To calm this argument, battle data were codified to develop realistic theories and bases for "realistic" games. The result of this effort to theorize and add realism was an enormous rule-learning challenge to the would-be game participant. This huge rule-learning requirement led to the formation in 1874 of a new school of war gaming referred to as free *kriegspiel* [11] which relied completely upon experienced umpires with no rule book. Within the game an effort was made to formulate the teams with special skills to eliminate the need for logistics and political data. Thereafter, war games were identified as either free or rigid, depending upon the role of the umpire. The two schools maintained a lively rivalry and, by each adopting the advantages of the other, seemed to improve the state-of-the-art of military gaming.

[11] German (*krieg*-war, *spiel*-game), a game for practicing or teaching military strategy of tactics.

The growth and development of war gaming have some very interesting parallels with developments in business gaming. In the beginning the senior generals were skeptical about the usefulness of gaming experience on the battlefield. The prime method used to convince these generals was to involve them in an exercise and then rely upon them to act as umpires in later war games; a successful tactic, too, for converting senior faculty members to today's potential of gaming. After games had become a part of the European military curriculum and were more and more sophisticated to include logistics and political information, they came under attack for training junior officers in the role of generals. It was argued that putting a subaltern in such a lofty position would spoil him for the normal menial lieutenant tasks. These arguments were rebutted by emphasizing the perspective such experience would provide. It was argued that the opportunity to see how each task fits into the overall scheme would emphasize why the timely completion of the task was important and would, simultaneously, improve the officer's decision-making habits. Little data were offered by each side in the argument; however, war gaming seems to have expanded during the era of this debate. Similar arguments have been raised against business gaming with about the same result.

A third debate in war gaming circles was between the theorists and the pragmatists. The increased use of mathematical models as a guide to executing certain military maneuvers, especially in coordination with field artillery, had a pronounced influence on war game design. This development raised a wave of criticism against the game environment as being too theoretical, with the resultant training experience producing an unrealistically trained officer. Unfortunately, a prime war game design response was to cloak the models with reams of data gathered on past wars to make them seem realistic. This ultimately made the game so cumbersome and unteachable that the free *kriegspiel* movement developed. It would appear that the designers lost sight of their purpose in gaming—training decision makers to develop habits of thought.

Student involvement seems to depend upon the amount of control the individual has in the simulated environment.[12] Evidence for this point was obtained from the arguments for the development of free *kriegspiel* citing the lack of enthusiasm and understanding on the part of students in the large games of the day.[13] On the basis of war game experience, therefore, to engender conscientious businesslike plans, the student must feel his decisions dominate the structure of the model. Thus, the economic models for gaming should be fairly flexible ones that respond to the decisions of the players, and the emphasis in model design should be on understandable cause-effect relationships which can normally be discerned during the play. These relationships should be defined consistent with what is known or generally assumed about cause-effect phenomena in the real world, but need not be derived from real data. The degree of verisimilitude of the model is important only to convince the student of the businesslike qualities of the simulated environment and to prevent misinterpretations of known phenomena.

A critical element to the success of a war game in fulfilling its teaching objectives was the effectiveness of the umpire.[14] The umpire or administrator is just as critical to a business game. A well-designed game generates a strong student motivation to win. The desire to win can be quite a disruptive force, as it prevents experimentation with new approaches and dominates student discussions to the exclusion of considering the decision-making process. This desire can be moderated by judicious guidance during the play encouraging the students to consider the causes of their moves and to experiment with improving their decision-making ability. Such student efforts are reinforced by a concluding session which provides a comparative evaluation of the participant's plans. The challenge to the umpire in the concluding session is to generate a discussion which compares the decision-making approaches of the participants and de-emphasizes the outcome of the exercise.

[12] G. J. Thomas, *The Genesis and Practice of Operational Gaming,* p. 78.
[13] Farrand Sayre, *Map Maneuvers,* p. 17.
[14] J. P. Young, "A Survey of War Games," pp. 19–20.

Concluding Remarks

Considering the war game heritage and early business game experience, the two main challenges to the game developer are: (1) to develop an exercise which is simple enough to be understood at the start, yet complex enough to challenge the experienced participant; and (2) to develop the game environment so that rational play can generate interesting managerial problems of increasing complexity. Recent game experience would indicate that both of these problems have been solved in large part by appropriately timed faculty support and guidance. A simulation model must be fairly complex to provide adequate data for a graduate student to search for decision-making opportunities and experiment with analytical techniques. Such a complex environment presents a significant introductory problem to the student who is learning the rules of the simulated environment. It is imperative for the student to have a prompt mastery of the rules in order that he may believe in his control of the destiny of his firm. Such a belief generates a sincere application of the student's decision-making skills and the appropriate sense of involvement. The attainment of such involvement is heavily dependent upon adequate faculty awareness of the information needs of each student and the appropriate responses to these needs.

The participants' decisions for their firms provide the future data and environment of play for their next managerial problems. To obtain a worthwhile learning experience, these problems should require thorough analysis based on prior simulated and curriculum experience, at a continuously demanding rate. The most effective approach that has been found is to create a game in which the faculty functions as a natural part of the simulated environment. This allows the faculty to make assignments and pose questions to the students inducing them to prepare a broad range of analysis which can exploit the learning opportunities in the game. The assumption of such a role by the faculty involves an awareness of the opportunities in the environment and the cumulative nature of gaming. In essence, gaming requires a more continuous form of faculty support than most teaching approaches.

A theme of this study is that to implement a business game for management development successfully, the game must be designed by the faculty involved for the needs of a particular group of students. Management development is very much an art and, as such, dependent upon careful guidance from experienced individuals. The cumulative nature of gaming emphasizes this dependence as it requires a completed course design before the start of the exercise. Creating such a design, with a heterogeneous group of faculty, requires a considerable gestation period to develop concepts of the faculty profitably in the game environment for a given student body. If a game represents these interests, there is no problem in involving the faculty adequately nor in challenging the most sophisticated of students. The potential of present gaming rests in part on the ease of its modification to the specific audience. Experience at the Harvard Business School is offered as evidence.

The remainder of this monograph is an account of the development, status, and use of a business game in management development. Chapter II is an account of how one particular business game evolved over a nine-year period to its present state. In part, this chapter is an exposition of failures to indicate why some phases of business activity are not included in the present simulation. Chapter III is a detailed explanation of the simulated environment to serve as a reference for individuals utilizing the model or to provide an interested individual an account of what the model can and cannot do in order to appraise its appropriateness for his curriculum. Chapter IV on Game Design describes the elements necessary to implement a game for management development. Chapter V on Recent Gaming Experience includes a description of the game as part of a two-week course, as a laboratory for implementing economic strategy with senior executives, and two successful methods of using the game in an MBA curriculum. The final chapter (Chapter VI) concerns the research that has been conducted on this game in the curriculum at the Harvard Business School.

CHAPTER II

The Evolution of the HBS Management Simulation Game

Gaming, as an approach to developing business-decision makers, has evolved quite rapidly in the last ten years from a flashy two-day exercise to a well-controlled, required course at several professional business schools. The pace of this evolution is the product of a great deal of experimentation with gaming in management development and the rapid acceptance of gaming in a wide variety of programs. Game experimentation seems to have been stimulated by the interdisciplinary aspects of business games and the intense involvement the process generates within the students. The high degree of student involvement, a prime purpose of utilizing games, is a pervasive influence which can be a disruptive force if not properly channeled to complement the curriculum. Thus, game experimentation has focused upon how one can successfully channel student gaming effort to improve the total learning experience in a professional school. It has been an iterative process of selecting learning goals, creating a game design, and evaluating the results in order to reselect goals. The following description traces one family of simulation models through a series of games to illustrate this process of experimentation. A purpose of this description is to afford the reader a historical perspective on the present state of gaming in order that the experimentation can be carried on more effectively.

Gaming experiments at the Harvard Business School were started by borrowing an existing simulation model—the UCLA Model #3—and by creating a game tailored to the HBS–MBA Program. Adapting a working simulation model allows a faculty to obtain gaming experience quickly without the costly commitment of model development. However, models include the biases of their designers which, as more encompassing games are developed, may prove inhibiting to the attainment of a game's full learning potential. As the present method of gaming has been influenced by the UCLA strain of models, in order to provide the reader with a complete understanding of the HBS Simulation Model and the approach used, a description of early gaming efforts at UCLA is included. The intent of this complete description of one strain of games is to provide background to obtain a better understanding of the potential of business gaming for developing decision makers.

This account of UCLA and HBS gaming documents the evolution of business gaming from its inception to the present day. The first stage of gaming was concerned with testing the feasibility of involving mature decision makers in a simulated economic environment as described in the development of the UCLA #1 game. This notion is supported by the first few publications on business gaming, wherein a great deal of credence is given to enthusiastic responses of experienced managers on the realism and the meaningfulness of the game.[1] The development of the next two UCLA models focused more on how does one create simulation games which will involve and motivate mature individuals in an educational environment. The report of the Kansas Business Game Conference held during this period describes several instances where the game involvement was not for involvement's sake; and it shows how the game could meaningfully be channeled to supplement the curriculum and add a new dimension to business training.[2] The most recent phase of business gaming is concerned with searching for improved methods of implementing meaningful games as adjuncts to ongoing curricula which involve considering

[1] McDonald and Ricciardi, "The Business Decision Game," pp. 140–142. A. N. Schrieber, "Gaming a New Way to Teach Business Decision Making," pp. 18–29.

[2] *Proceedings of the National Symposium on Management Games.*

the implications for both the curriculum and the game. This phase was codified at the Tulane Conference on Games and it is reflected in the comprehensive development of the Carnegie Tech Game as well as the efforts at Harvard.[3]

Consider the year 1956 as the point of departure for this study. Operational gaming has been in existence for ten years. Computers with limited memory and computing speeds were available. UCLA was fortunate to have a number of people with both war gaming and economic modeling experience.

Development of the First Simulation Model

The initiators of the first game had been developing simulation models to investigate logistics problems in the Management Science Research Project at UCLA. In the fall of 1956 the Research Project was given access to an IBM 650 computer. Dr. Tibor Fabian along with Dr. J. R. Jackson, stimulated in part by the acquisition of a new computer and challenged with teaching an undergraduate economics course, decided to develop an economic simulation game. Their teaching objectives for the first model were:

(1) To demonstrate the basic economic concepts.
(2) To give the students an appreciation of how to perform a marginal analysis in a dynamic environment.

The initial model was crude by today's standards. Only five firms could compete in the industry with one product each. They were faced with only five decisions: Price, Advertising, Research and Development, Production Volume, and Purchase or Sale of Capital Equipment. The accounting statement reported only gross figures for the firm. Yet the initial games with classes of 45 students induced the students to spend hours of time in analysis to determine marginal costs and market elasticities. The game was so successful it was decided to experiment with MBA students to evaluate the potential of the game as a laboratory for decision making.

[3] W. R. Dill et al., *Conference on Business Games.*

MBA Trial Runs

Three simulation sessions were conducted in the fall of 1957 to provide the students with a management planning experience. The pedagogic objective of the sessions was to evaluate the potential of the game as a laboratory for decision making. The designers agreed that Model #1 was too simple and artificial, but there was great uncertainty as to how it should be improved. On the basis of experience with the simulation during the summer of 1957, it seemed desirable to have an introductory session which included a few practice moves prior to the simulation session. This would separate the rule-learning session from the game proper, and the faculty could encourage students in the practice session to experiment and learn how to operate as managers of the simulated firms without lasting consequences to their firms. Over the years, experiments have been conducted with alternative methods of introducing a game, but no better method than scheduling a practice move has been found.

Student and faculty assessment of the gaming sessions was very favorable. In spite of the limited range of decisions and the artificiality of the data, the MBA students became quite involved in the game and carried out a thorough analysis of a dynamic situation which contributed to a greater student understanding of the process of planning. It was concluded that it was feasible and desirable to involve MBA students in a simulation game. In addition, these sessions identified aspects of the model which could be improved. Examples of shortcomings are as follows:

(1) The demand function was not elastic in a realistic manner to varying budgets.
(2) There was no means for expanding production quickly for a short period.
(3) The forms were not very readable and did not conform to reasonable managerial accounting practices.
(4) Allowing decisions in discrete steps was unrealistic and detracted from the game (prices had been restricted to 10-cent steps).

UCLA Simulation Game #2

In addition to the output and rule limitations of the original teaching model, the objectives of the first simulation game seemed too restrained for use in an MBA program. The experience of the early simulations indicated that one important potential of gaming was to place the individual in a decision-making group for a period of time. This gave him an opportunity to experience the problems of communication and working in an organization. A second student experience that gaming created was that of searching and evaluating the usefulness of information. The experimentation with Model #1 led to a more pertinent set of feasible MBA objectives for a simulated environment. These were defined as: (1) to provide a dynamic planning experience in a businesslike environment; (2) to involve the students in a decision-making group; and (3) to offer an information search program for a set of decisions under uncertainty.

Model #2, as well as Model #1, was designed to be strongly related to economic intuition as this was felt to be important in creating interest and also in making it possible to explain a complex decision-making simulation reasonably quickly.[4] The market mechanism and the cost mechanisms were described in general terms in the instructions and were founded upon basic economic principles, not of any specific industry, but principles which seem to be qualitatively true of many industries. It would have been desirable to have more data to induce organization of the task, but it was felt a game could be designed to proceed quickly and this would induce the players to specialize with a paucity of available data.

A goal of game designers in creating a model for management development is to have the players make their decisions for their firm under uncertainty. In order to have meaningful comparative discussions, however, it is desirable to eliminate true chance factors. The elimination of random elements provides a useful basis for discussion among firms in the concluding session. In experimenting with the development of Model #2, it was found that an effective state of uncertainty could be created by: (1) the variabil-

[4] J. R. Jackson, "Learning from Experience in Business Games," p. 101.

ity of total market with firm activities; (2) the existence of an economic growth factor in the market; (3) variability of total market and of market share with the behavior of industry as a whole; and (4) the impossibility of completely unraveling the cause effect relationships in the model during the play because of sophisticated modeling techniques.[5] Such procedures are valid today. It is important that the players be able to understand at the conclusion of the game why the economic responses happened—at least qualitatively. This allows them to evaluate their own activities and to consider their planning experience in light of alternative players' activity.

First Uses of Model #2

The game that utilized Model #2 was designed to involve a rapid style of play with moves about every 15 minutes to attain the aforementioned objectives. It was felt that the game would involve firms of from three to five participants. A game session included a 20-minute introduction followed by three practice decisions on Friday with the game session scheduled all day Saturday. It was suggested to the students that a brief written statement concerning their goals and policies might aid the success of their firms. The gaming credo of the time seemed to be minimum interference with student performance in the simulated environment, since any interference might inhibit student involvement and abort the objectives of the exercise. As more gaming experience was accumulated, this credo proved absolutely wrong. Assignments, if in consonance with the simulated environment, seem to induce more conscientious involvement and do not detract from the objectives. In fact, assignments are essential if the exercise is to achieve its potential as a learning experience.

A class was divided into firms competing in several industries simultaneously to provide a comparative discussion, at the conclusion of play, on how industries differed owing to the varied tactics of the firms. Typically a six-hour simulated session would achieve four simulated years' experience which would be followed by a one-hour discussion of the planning activity of the firms.

[5] *Ibid.*, p. 100.

Each firm was given a half hour at the conclusion of play to prepare an evaluation statement of its own activities, to define wherein it thought it did well, and how it used the available information. The administrators of the game created a series of charts showing the sales, profits, and price movements of each industry and of each firm within the industry. The comparative discussion is pertinent and can generate interest in why the industries differ even though they are identical in their basic economic structure, but always will develop uniquely owing to the behavior of the individual firm's responses to the environment and to competition. This difference provides a starting point for discussing the various strategies the firms attempted to implement.

Conclusions on Game #2 Experience

The sessions did involve the students in a dynamic decision-making problem which was in part due to their own decisions as well as to the modeled environment. Through the game, students seemed to achieve an appreciation of the influence of problem definition and the choice of information in the planning process. They did obtain an experience in working with a decision-making group under pressure. The accounting statements provided an interesting search problem in considering what information was pertinent and how to operate given the limited time available. By providing a planning environment and forcing small groups to select information from a set accounting statement, ostensibly the stated teaching environment objectives, a planning experience through gaming was achieved.[6]

The success of the UCLA #2 Model can be seen by the fact that as of 1964 it was still utilized in at least 14 institutions.[7] Because of expanded teaching objectives, several schools modified the rules of play to include a labor negotiation of production rates or they increased the output to expand the financial implications of external funds.[8] Model #2 is used in seven different courses but mainly as an adjunct to a General Management course.

[6] *Ibid.*, p. 96.

[7] Dale and Klasson, "Business Gaming," p. 40.

[8] Henshaw and Jackson, *The Executive Game.*

Comments indicate that the model itself has successfully accomplished its teaching goals of providing a dynamic problem and presenting the students with an opportunity to obtain a planning experience in a short span of time. Concluding sessions seem best when the topics to be discussed are identified at the beginning of the session. These topics include proper use of information, why one plan is more appropriate than another, how certain kinds of information can be improved upon, and how to evaluate different forms of analysis. The purpose of the concluding session is to show how better use could have been made of the available information.[9]

However, the restricted analysis opportunity which Model #2 offered, limited its use with advanced students to the rapid decision style of play thereby decreasing its learning potential. A careful analysis of from four to six periods of data is adequate to provide a basis for a successful strategy, and the students often lose interest in further analysis. Encouraging organization and delegation of responsibility in a firm can prove fruitless since the management problem does not pose that great a challenge to one individual. The style of student participation was typically a discussion of alternative goals and policies followed by a division of calculating tasks during the short-move sessions. What was desired was more analyzable data—thus a more complex simulated environment. It would have been feasible with the IBM 650 computer, but not economical.

The Development of UCLA Model #3

The restraint of computation capacity on the creation of realistic and challenging games was removed in the winter of 1959 when an IBM 709 computer became available. By this time the UCLA group had two years of gaming experience and had some definite ideas on what a good management game should include. Professor J. R. Jackson and colleagues were encouraged to develop a game on the 709 for use in an Engineering Management short course.

A prime concern of the designers was to provide a problem

[9] J. R. Jackson, "Learning from Experience in Business Games," p. 104.

complex enough to encourage specialization which would require a hierarchical organization of the simulated firm's managers. The new model included more specific kinds of quantitative data that required the students to make detailed analyses of the market, to identify production costs, and to consider financial alternatives over an extended period of simulated time. The cost structure of former models was very simple, but, with the capacity of the large machine, costs of operation in the simulation were generated in a more realistic manner in response to decisions by the firm. The complex model allowed the game to extend over several days which improved the learning potential considerably. The new game was planned to proceed either one move per day for a two-week short course, or one move per week over a period of from 10 to 16 weeks. This program would allow the participants to make a thorough analysis of the simulation output and carefully plan for each move.

The teaching objectives of the new model were an expanded version of the objectives of Model #2. In some ways these objectives reflected what seemed feasible to teach about the "planning experience" through gaming. The objectives were as follows: [10]

(1) To provide a dynamic planning experience in a business environment.
(2) To involve the student in a decision-making group made up of specialists.
(3) To provide an information search problem for a set of decision makers under uncertainty.
(4) To provide adequate data for a detailed analysis and development of functional plans.

It was felt the participants should have as much freedom as possible in forming their firm organizations. To accomplish this freedom, a prime design criteria of the model had been to require an equal amount of student analysis for managing either a product or a functional area, such as marketing. The workload requirements for either method of organization were seemingly balanced by allowing each firm to produce up to three products and to have

[10] One may observe they were very general, since the developers were not willing to commit themselves to specific activities.

roughly equal quantities of data on the financial, marketing, and production aspects of the firm. To reinforce this flexibility, the accounting statements provided were organized in such a manner that the firms could divide the data either functionally or by product. The flexible design concept has proved to be very desirable and is common to most gaming models today. However, merely providing equal amounts of data is not adequate; the game play must continuously create a challenging problem to all specialists, which UCLA #3 does not.

The model and the rules for manipulating it continued the theme of encouraging the participant to observe his own learning by experience in order to improve his learning ability. Thus, a prime function of the simulation was to give the individuals in the firm prompt feedback on the implication of their decisions in such a manner that they could perceive how they were acquiring expertise in the environment. The time span remained a quarter, and all decisions had an immediate, as well as future, impact.

The instructions did not spell out specific cost relationships, and most data were aggregated to force the student to search out the specific cost relationships and demand responses in the simulated environment. For example, indirect costs of changing production were not spelled out, but by careful analysis could be derived. These costs were not made explicit to encourage the student to make a continual analysis of his reports in light of his decisions to derive meaningful estimates of costs and market response. The lack of explicit information, but having it implicitly available, seemed to be one method of providing a dynamic business problem which could be solved by careful observation and analysis. It was assumed that careful faculty coaching or coordination with the game would induce such analysis. This lack of specificity caused trouble in later runs when more specific assignments were given.

The main new feature of the simulation was an industry report which summarized industry activity. In earlier games, experiments with industry data had proved they were important to the competitive aspects of the game, since these data gave members of each firm an indication of the marketing strategy and the economic status of their competitors. Such reports had proved very useful in assisting the firms to develop a strategy. A second piece of information found useful in early games was an economic index for use in forecasting. Thus, the report also contained a business index which was a pertinent measure of the general economic conditions of the industry. Including the information in the industry report seemed to reinforce the common knowledge flavor of the data.

The designers tested the model with a few faculty members and graduate students and received enthusiastic accolades. The game seemed ready to use as planned for the two-week Engineering Management course and was scheduled as an afternoon 1½ hour class which would meet each day for one move. The accounting reports were to be available to each firm at the start of the class, and a decision was due at the completion. Because of time restrictions the game was not introduced by a practice session; instead, four quarters of prior operating reports for each firm were given to the members of the firm the evening before the start of the program.

As a management simulation game the design was a success; as a meaningful course the session was a debacle. The failure may have been attributable to lack of scheduled time in the program to allow the participants to deal adequately with the simulation game. The game administrators assumed because the students were engineers and accustomed to dealing with abstractions, they would readily understand the simulated environment and could deal with the problem with just an introductory discussion and without the practice move. It was further assumed that, because the faculty groups of two or three had devised and carried out a workable plan in two hours or less per move, during the trial sessions surely four or five engineers could accomplish the task in less. Both assumptions proved false.

In Model #3, as in most complex games, there is a mass of detailed information to be assimilated for operating effectively as a firm. The process of assimilation requires time and assistance. The result of not providing adequate assistance or allowing enough time creates a great deal of frustration and bitter complaints from the students. In this instance, the engineers were very intrigued by the simulation and were highly motivated to attempt to work out plans and a strategy. Unfortunately they were not given proper time to learn or time to execute a decent analysis. After about five moves, most firms merely filled out the decision forms by pure hunch and considered the exercise a game. Comments indicated that the experience did communicate the significance of interdependency of functions in a firm, but the planning experience seemed slim. It is imperative for success to allow adequate time in the beginning of any simulation game session. This caution is still pertinent today. Most initial gaming attempts suffer from a schedule which allows insufficient time at the beginning of the exercise. Rule learning is a necessary procedure which must be scheduled as an integral part of a game.

Effective Uses of Model #3

In subsequent sessions where the participants were given an adequate amount of indoctrination and time to prepare decent decisions, Model #3 has proved to be an effective teaching experience. Its use was not as widespread as Model #2, because the large-scale computer was not available in as many different places as the medium-sized computer. This induced a new method of use, that of conducting a session by correspondence between various schools and the Western Data Processing Center. The first such correspondence took place with the University of California, Berkeley, in the spring of 1959, and the second was an interschool simulation game between Stanford, UCLA, San Diego State, and Southern California. The most common use of this improved model has been as an adjunct to a General Management course.

Early Gaming in the HBS–MBA Program

In the spring of 1961 UCLA Model #3 was used in a game at the Harvard Business School as an experiment in integrating the notions of organizational behavior and production management. The following teaching objectives were defined for guiding the development of the game:

(1) To demonstrate the interrelationship of functional decisions in a firm.
(2) To make the students more aware of the behavioral aspects of decision making.

(3) To demonstrate the relationship of production policies to production plans.
(4) To involve the students in a small organizational decision-making experience extended over a time with set requirements.

A class of ninety students enrolled in both courses was divided into three industries of six firms each. The game consisted of an introductory class, one discussion session on planning, a concluding session, and twelve moves in the simulated environment over an eight-week period. A pair of examinations on planning precepts was given to the class and each industry had been organized in a different manner to obtain data for evaluating the potential of gaming in the MBA curriculum. The experimental design results are discussed in Chapter VI. The data did support the use of gaming and provided a basis for an improved game for the following year.

The session appeared to have attained its goals of providing a production planning experience but was not too effective in integrating the two courses. However, the student response was sufficient to warrant continued experimentation. The experience indicated:

(1) A simulation game is a desirable addition to the curriculum but needs to be better adapted to the environment of the first-year MBA Program.
(2) It would seem more appropriate for all first-year courses rather than as an adjunct to just one pair.
(3) Greater emphasis in the classroom on analysis and a required written comment on the activities of the firm in the game seemed desirable.
(4) There is need for more detailed simulation data for specific functional areas to better relate the game to classwork.

1962 Simulation Developments

On the basis of the first run, the decision was made to continue experimenting with gaming in the first year of the MBA Program. It was felt there were two alternatives for improving the game for the students, either requiring more reports or making the model more "realistic." To gain further experience, two separate classes of ninety men were enrolled in a game. One class was required to submit more written comments during the session and the other was to deal with a more complex simulated environment.

In developing the game it seemed desirable to maintain similar introduction requirements for both classes to provide an equitable basis for comparison. The first series of moves was identical for both classes with the increase in the simulation complexity to occur during the play for the one class. The model revision increased the available cost data on the simulated firm and required more detailed decisions within the framework of the original simulation firm. The intent of the modelers was to disaggregate all variables one level; for example, product quality decisions were one fixed budget at the start. This budget had to be more specifically defined after move six by prescribing the quality of raw material in dollar amounts and the amount of labor per product. Similar new decisions were allowed for in the marketing and in the financial phases. The model responded to the aggregation of the new decisions exactly as it had before. However, now there were more data to base decisions on with resultant added flexibility in controlling the operation of the firm. The new model was designed so the firms could build up experience in the UCLA #3 Model and transfer this experience to the new environment.

The alternative approach to enrichment of the game was designed to require more reports and analyses of the given data as the session continued. As an example, after move four a four-quarter cash flow budget was submitted with each decision set. Similar additional reports were required starting with decisions six and eight. The intention of both teaching plans was to create a more meaningful learning experience for the participants by providing improved bases for classroom discussions on the simulation game activities. The discussions were to attempt to relate game analysis and decision making where pertinent to the course material and, it was hoped, to enrich both the game and the course.

On the basis of HBS Faculty observation of the different procedures, enrichment by additional reports during the sessions seemed far more effective. The reports required the student to analyze what he was doing and made the Faculty more aware of what was happening in the simulation. The students experimented with analytical techniques with the game data to complete the reports which provided a basis for classroom discussions in the various courses. The conclusion of this comparison supports the experience of war gaming that, given a simulation game, more time should be spent on how to use an environment than on a continued enrichment by effort in modeling.

Providing more detailed data which seemed more tractable to analytical techniques did not seem to involve the students or induce them to make better analyses as the game progressed, nor did it stimulate much classroom discussion. There was no observable data explaining whether the lack of success was due to how the complexity was introduced or to the feasibility of enriching this simulation in progress.[11] The participants seemed to view the changes in the simulation as creating a new environment and did not transfer the experience of their initial decisions to the enlarged model. The firms that had achieved a functioning group adjusted to the new environment and were able to adapt better to the larger numbers of decisions. The firms that had difficulty obtaining a working relationship and were not coping adequately with their simulated firms gave up and let one or two individuals attempt to carry the load. Thus, the successful firms had an improved learning experience by being exposed to two forms of a simulation but unfortunately the weak firms tended to play it as a game and lost interest thereby creating an uncomfortable morale problem. The positive result of the enriched model was the availability of more specific data without too many new rules for the participants.

Conclusions Resulting from the 1962 Game Sessions

A second evaluation experiment was designed to provide data on the appropriate teaching objectives for a game in an MBA curriculum. The design, discussed in Chapter VI, provided a set of bench marks for evaluation of the potential of the simulation

[11] Professor Schrieber successfully enriches the game he uses three times during each game session at the University of Washington, School of Business Administration.

session. The following precepts were proposed as definitions for which a game might provide a better learning experience than the case method of instruction:

Goal Precepts

(1) Today's decisions affect tomorrow's environment.
(2) Plans or policies are a series of consistent decisions.
(3) Functional decisions of the firm are interrelated, e.g., production decisions affect marketing decisions.
(4) The time dimension is a strategic factor in most decisions and must be realistically accounted for when selecting alternative courses of action.
(5) Decision makers in a time-dependent environment subject to change should be aware of the relationships of measurable variables; e.g., a decision should not only determine levels or rate but the best direction of movement, in view of probable developments.

Organization Behavior Precepts

(6) Leadership functions in a small group do not have to be centralized but can appropriately be shifted at least informally along with shifts in the nature of the tasks, so as to capitalize on individual skills and interests.
(7) Integrating different points of view and areas of competence in accomplishing a common task is an important function.
(8) People react to alternatives emotionally on nonlogical grounds but attempt to cloak their reactions in logical arguments.
(9) A perceptive manager places less reliance on stereotyped solutions to organizational and human relation problems and gives greater recognition to different kinds of solutions which are appropriate in different circumstances at different times.

The precepts were quite useful in Faculty discussions on what was being attempted in the game and how it might be improved. It was concluded that the students in the simulation classes seemed to be better able to synthesize the various functions in an overall plan, that they seemed more aware of the relationships of measurable variables in a complex environment (rate of change, trend, etc.), and that they had a better grasp of the importance of the time dimension than the students without the simulation experience. There was a consensus that this simulation exercise provided an arena for making the students aware of the interrelationship of functions in an ongoing business and the importance not only of revising budgets and decision-making models but also of evaluating how the budget and models were constructed. The Faculty decided to introduce a management simulation game as a required part of the first-year Harvard Business School MBA course during 1962–1963.

Development of the 1963 HBS Simulation Game

The 1962 session had provided some insight into better coupling of the simulation to the curriculum. A large segment of the Faculty had been involved in the session as members of Boards of Directors of simulated firms. The Faculty members with no prior game experience felt that if they had engaged in a brief four- or five-move simulation prior to the student run they would have been better prepared. In addition, both sessions involved a number of teaching Faculty who felt that without much effort the enriched model could be slightly altered to accommodate their particular course objectives. Finally, reports to the Faculty on the progress of the game were not adequate to inform the Faculty associated with this simulation about what was happening without almost as much analysis as each student had to make within his own firm. The main thrust of the constructive comments was a request for more specific data on the operation of the simulated firm and more distilled data for the Faculty.

The 1963 simulation game shifted the philosophy of the game from one of general planning only to more functional analysis. The game was planned to simulate decision-making experiences similar to those of a financial, marketing, or production manager. Up to this time the focus of the game had been upon the decisions of the general manager. This emphasis had resulted in the aggregation of a number of costs and allowed the published rules for extracting costs from the model to be loosely defined. The functional requirement made it important that the simulation should include greater opportunity for specific tools of analysis. This opportunity always existed but it was not the prime design criterion of the simulation and although cost data were available in the economic model, they had not been in a particularly handy form in the accounting statements. The Faculty had not encouraged students to make specific kinds of analyses and, as a result, the students had up to this time spent most of their time on devising goals and analyzing the results for cost information, relying primarily on marginal analysis to select from alternatives. In addition, the instructions had purposely not been precise as to costs and the operation of the production function, in order that students would be required to make a careful analysis of the data and form their own conclusions. The new simulation had to reduce the time for analyzing vague data to allow the firms to see the results of using analytical tools during the simulation. Furthermore, the revised game required extensive instructions to provide students with a quick insight into how the costs of the model were generated.

The teaching objectives for the 1963 game were similar to those of 1962 but greater emphasis was given to the game activity as it related to the required first-year courses of the MBA Program. The following objectives were defined by the game committee:

(1) To integrate the first-year courses of Control, Finance, Marketing, Production, and Organizational Behavior.
(2) To create a dynamic planning problem which would extend overtime and provide data for the following participant activities:
  a. The definition of a forecasting model.
  b. The development of a long-range financial plan.
  c. The establishment of criteria for product profitability.
  d. The definition of a production scheduling rule.
(3) To provide a small group decision-making experience.

Rather than create an all-new model, it was decided to modify the UCLA #3 simulation and to revise the instructions more explicitly to identify costs and the simulated time delays that existed. This seemed not only the cheapest and most expeditious procedure, but also the one that offered a number of tactical advantages. First, the modeled market had intrigued a wide variety of students and seemed to be both stable and elastic. Second, the general relation of fixed to variable costs as well as the cost variations at various production levels were understandable, and the model had the potential for a decent financial problem. In addition, there were several members of the Faculty who had achieved some competence in dealing with the game and they understood the model. Finally, the Faculty were aware of the general nature of this particular simulation model and had some confidence in its potential.

The most noticeable changes in the model were the addition of several financial variables with the introduction of accounts receivable and the ability of a firm to borrow money by line of credit, short-term loans, and long-term loans. A stock price for each firm was developed based on profits, return on investment, dividends, and liabilities. The stock price was intended to be a financial appraisal of the firm, but no provision was made for buying or selling stock.

The market was modified by splitting each of the three demand determinants to create six forms of market influence differentiated by the time of impact. The parameters of the new determinants were modified to give each of the six firms in an industry one characteristic influence which was more effective than its competitors'. Thus, one firm's marketing budget would be more influential than the others, while product quality would generate proportionally more sales for another firm. Market information on this special sector was available to each firm at a price. The main addition to production was to identify more indirect costs on the accounting statements and to explain in the instructions both the costs and the time lags of production change. The only proposal finally rejected was the special market influence. It produced bizarre market results.

A trial game session, scheduled for the Faculty in November, was arranged to introduce the new simulation and to test the adequacy of the instructions. Involving the Faculty in a short game seemed to be the most effective manner to familiarize and indoctrinate the Faculty and to evaluate the model in regard to the first-year MBA courses. The game sessions involved some 41 Faculty members divided into two industries of four firms each. The stated purpose of the session was to familiarize all Faculty members teaching first-year classes with the decision-making problems associated with the simulation so that they could better accommodate the potential of the game session to their individual course. The trial run included an introductory session, one move per week for four weeks, a brief intermediary session with small groups of Faculty to insure understanding after two moves, and a concluding discussion with all participants to consider various teaching approaches.

The Faculty run started well but proved to be a little more motivating and involving than had been anticipated. The high level of involvement induced the Faculty firms to spend too much time on the competitive aspects of the game. Several firms attempted to develop a winning strategy in two moves and carry it out in two more. Their strategies proved infeasible primarily because the firms had to make a series of assumptions about market behavior which often proved false. A few individuals concluded that the simulation was not too realistic when, in four moves, the market did not respond to their strategy. Others, having spent up to eight hours per move, worried about the amount of student time required. The simulation was developed to require a minimum of ten to twelve moves to implement a strategy, and the Faculty run proved that four moves are far too few. The method of proof was a bit harassing to all and created a few problems. The experience did make most individuals aware of the model, the rules of play, and especially the importance of Faculty advisors to keep the students focused on the decision-making process rather than just on winning the game. It is vital that all Faculty members associated with a gaming session have some experience with a game. A more successful tactic for acquiring Faculty experience is discussed in Chapter IV.

The game was conducted, in the spring of 1963, as a decision-making laboratory for all first-year MBA students. It was a joint effort of all teaching in the required first-year curriculum. Written assignments were timed so that students could concentrate upon aspects of the simulation which were pertinent to specific classroom discussions in the various courses.

Conclusions Resulting from the 1963 Game Sessions

The first full-scale trial was a success from the accounts of both Faculty and students. The operating cost for a student body of 660 students excluding Faculty time was less than $1,200 of which almost a third was for paper for the output. An IBM 7090 computer at the educationally subsidized rate was utilized.

The one suggestion most common for improving the exercise was that the data were not available in the correct format nor was the vocabulary on the forms completely appropriate for integrating the game with the course and case material of the first-year curriculum. It seemed difficult to make assignments and follow-up reports that related to classroom activity and provided adequate detail. Some of these omissions were related to omissions in the instructions to participants and others to the form of the output.

An obvious conclusion from the 1963 experience was that there comes a time when a continued modification of an old simulation model can no longer be efficient. Significant elements in deciding when to change the model are the timeliness of the vocabulary, the format of the simulation output, and the state of the instructions. On the basis of experience with this model, an essential characteristic of a simulation for effective integration with a curriculum appears to be the vocabulary of the output and the functional forms of the model. It is difficult to utilize a simulation activity unless it uses a similar vocabulary and provides data in the level of detail considered in the courses. For example, when considering alternative methods of financing acceptable financial ratios, tax benefits, and accounting practices must be available in the data to allow the students to implement the methods they were exposed to in class. Furthermore, these data should be labeled consistent with the vocabulary used in the classroom to facilitate discussion. Game sessions proved that detailed cost data on the simulated firm were required and disclosed that the specificity such data must have is sometimes underestimated.

Starting with an established model to obtain gaming experience is an efficient approach. The bulk of time up to 1963 had been spent on how to use the simulation model and what modifications should be made to the game to improve its learning potential. From this experience, a sound repertoire of possible gaming activities was developed for use in designing a new game.

Tactical Problems of Game Design

During the three years of research on implementation, several problems plagued the designers. These problems, somewhat unique to gaming, are not obvious when initiating a game effort. An unresolved game design issue is how much should controllable costs, the duration time lags of budget influences, and normal economic behavior of the model be identified and explained to the participants.

Basically the goal of the designer is to stimulate the student to deduce the costs, time responses, and elasticities of the simulated environment. The instructions to the game serve to give the student confidence in his ability to make a successful thorough analysis. The Faculty role in introducing a game is to explain that the instructions are but a sample of the total available information. The challenge to the participants is in the analysis of the feedback data to appraise the critical elements of the simulated environment for developing a profitable plan.

The uncertain quantum is how much information to provide in the instructions to obtain student momentum yet not too much that it overwhelms him and inhibits his search of the feedback data. A detailed compendium encourages the student to rely too heavily upon the rule book to understand the simulated environment. This induces habits of response learning, not data search and analysis, which are most desirable to business gaming experience. The goal, therefore, is to create a challenging model and set of instructions that will give the student adequate support to meet the challenge of searching for causes of appropriate responses in the simulated environment. Clever modeling can allow a significant portion of the causes to derive from competitors' activities.

A method which did not prove too successful was to provide in the simulation adequate data for the implementation of a specific technique. In this particular case, the game was intended to provide a follow-up exercise in the use of the production scheduling rule as developed by Holt, Muth, Modigliani, and Simon.[12] After discussing the rule in a Production class, an assignment was made to develop the parameters for using a linear decision rule in scheduling the production of each firm. Few firms performed successful analyses, and the assignment created an undesirable student reaction. Providing data in an explicit format to be manipulated by a given rule was resented by the students as unrealistic and was considered by them as an exercise. The students became identified with the control of their firm and wanted to manage as they saw fit. Therefore it seemed more appropriate to provide a wealth of data on overtime hiring costs, to encourage the students to pursue their own particular method of decision making, and to require each firm to make this method explicit in a written assignment. Teaching specific techniques in a general management game is not as effective as other methods of instruction.

Finally a word about functional balance. It is important to insure that all phases of the simulation consist of equally critical problems in order that comparable work loads and interesting jobs may result for the various functions involved in the operation of the firm. In the 1962–1963 simulation, the successful firms soon acquired more than adequate funds which made the financial planning trivial. What compounded the problem was that the costs were formulated in such a manner that those firms that did get into large debt had to restrict their operation and plan very carefully to obtain a good financial position; they more often did not and gave up on the job. The financial aspects of the game resulted in stimulating too little analysis and also detracted from the attainment of the teaching objectives. To maintain a good level of analysis, the managerial problems had to continue their challenge throughout the game.

Conclusions

The power of management gaming rests on the ability of the approach to involve the student completely in a businesslike environment. This involvement is largely dependent on the prompt feed-

[12] C. Holt et al., *Planning Production, Inventories, and Work Force.*

back on the student's decision making. To make this involvement a continuous challenge, the student manager and his competitors should strongly influence the environment. Early experiences have indicated that this policy is best implemented through the simulation model. One of the strengths of the early model and the one that has been developed is synthesizing the firms' marketing decisions to create a market which is unique to the particular sequence of recent decisions. Thus, the simulated environment is a composite of each student's activities, of his competitors, and of the model. The economic activity of the firm quickly reflects the student's influence, and the student identifies very strongly with the firm's results. This process generates a very responsible attitude in the participant. This is what makes business gaming so effective as a teaching approach.

CHAPTER III

The Present Simulation Model

After three years of experimentation with the UCLA model, a new model specifically tailored to a professional MBA curriculum was developed in the summer of 1963. It required seven man-months of effort to create a new completely documented modular computer model. Since that time, this simulation model with minor changes has been successfully used as the basis of a game adjunct to the HBS–MBA Program and the Advanced Management Program. The Faculty, satisfied with the simulation and its use in a management game, has shifted developmental efforts to experimentation with materials and assignments to best supplement the simulation. A discussion of the use of the simulation is presented in the following chapter. The detailed discussion in this chapter is provided for use as a reference to understand how the simulation operates. This background information is important to those developing a game and to Faculty members serving as advisors in a game using the model.

The general scheme of the simulation is presented first to provide some perspective for a comprehensive discussion of the economic model and the rules for manipulating this model. The rationale and characteristics of the marketing, production, and financial aspects of the simulation will then be discussed. The economic relationships have been emphasized, but the functional form of these relationships on intuitive grounds has only briefly been defended. This method has been used to focus on exactly what exists in the simulation. A teacher considering this simulation as an aid should play a trial game for a few moves to achieve the feeling of realism and to perceive how the factors in the model behave. In other words, this discussion should afford some understanding of how the simulation operates so a teacher can develop an appropriate assignment and better introduce students to the rules.

The model is presently used at the Harvard Business School as part of a simulation game which is a laboratory adjunct to the MBA curriculum and a three-week exercise in an Advanced Management Program. The general goal of this game in the MBA curriculum is to develop the student's ability in problem solving, including discovering, analyzing, and weighing the significant factors of a business problem, and deciding on an operational course of action. To operate successfully the student must devise a suitable plan for a course of action with a decision-making organization and implement it in a dynamic environment. The economic model was developed to encourage students to use the concepts they have been exposed to in their course work, namely, analyzing the data and selecting alternative courses of action.

The specific MBA teaching objectives that guided the design of this simulation are:

(1) To integrate the concepts and experience of the first-year MBA courses.
(2) To provide an opportunity for the students to use the analytic approaches they have been exposed to in static environments in a dynamic uncertain environment.
(3) To involve the students in a clinical organizational behavioral experience in which each individual is required to set goals, establish policies, and carry out a plan in coordination with other individuals.
(4) To give the students the experience of creating an operational plan and implementing this plan in an environment which evaluates the appropriateness of the plan.

The Overall Design of the Simulation

The simulation was developed to allow a four-man or five-man team to manage a complete business. As designed, this simulation represents the economic aspects of manufacturing, financing,

EXHIBIT 1

Management Simulation
Income Statement for a Typical Firm

I N D U S T R Y 41 F I R M 1

I N C O M E S T A T E M E N T P E R I O D 6

TOTAL SALES REVENUE		$ 2960331.
COST OF GCODS SOLC		
FABRICATION LABCR	381543.	
ASSEMBLY LABOR	333208.	
RAW MATERIALS	427063.	
PURCHASED PARTS	157327.	
OVERTIME PREMIUM	0.	1299141.
G R O S S P R O F I T		1661190.
FACTCRY CVERHEAD		
INDIRECT LABOR	38721.	
SUPERVISION	143241.	
MAINTENANCE	107081.	
DEPRECIATION	52390.	341433.
SELLING AND ADMINISTRATIVE EXPENSES		
MARKETING	425000.	
PROMOTION	50000.	

```
    COMMISSIONS ANC SALESMENS EXPENSE       202016.
    WAREHOUSE AND SHIPPING                   66207.
    MARKET RESEARCH                              0.
    PRODUCT DEVELOPMENT                     100000.
    ADMINISTRATIVE                           83130.              926353.

OPERATING PROFIT                                                 393404.

INTEREST EXPENSE                                                  25489.
SECURITY INCOME                                                       0.
TAXABLE INCOME                                                   367915.
INCOME TAX                                                       191316.

N E T   I N C O M E                                      $       176599.

          P L A N T   R E P O R T

PLANT CAPACITY, PERIOD   7                $ 2568205.
LOSS FROM DEPRECIATION                        64205.
GAIN FROM NEW INVESTMENT                          0.
PLANT CAPACITY, PERIOD   8                $ 2503999.

TOTAL NUMBER OF EMPLOYEES                       864.

          B U S I N E S S   I N D E X (SEASONALLY ADJUSTED)

     PERIODS  3 TO  6 (ACTUAL)         650       636       654       675
     PERIODS  7 TO 10 (ESTIMATED)      680       682       666       662
     PERIODS 11 TO 14 (ESTIMATED)      668       693       694       700
```

and selling in a consumer goods industry. A modest amount of reality was included to allow an instructor, during the introduction of rules, to refer to a real-life industrial situation. The price structure of the goods available for sale in the simulation is similar to the traffic appliance industry where the allowable, feasible product prices range between $4.00 and $44.00.[1] The production facilities of the model can be considered a generalization of appliance manufacturing operations, since the relationship of capital investment to employees is similar. Such facilities include relatively unskilled labor force working in fabrication and assembly departments. The financial aspects of the modeled firm represent a medium-sized publicly held firm with assets of $4 million to $6 million and annual normal operating profits of $400,000 to $600,000. Such a size firm would probably employ four to five managers, not be financially secure, and require aggressive business plans to survive. Exhibit 1 is an income statement for a typical firm. The simulation operates by manipulating the rules through 12 iterations to develop a dynamic imitation of the economic activity of each firm for the decision period which is defined as a quarter of a year.

Attempts have been made to develop a simulation which would require about ten hours of total student time per firm per move in the initial stages. This time requirement, coupled with an intended style of play to allow only three hours between acquisition of firm reports and submission of firm decision, is to induce the firms to organize so that each member of the firm becomes a specialist. Each firm receives five copies of its reports in an information structure which allows variety in forms of organization. The firms are also encouraged to organize to best fit their talents. Firm organization and the resultant specialization are important aspects of the simulation as they generate an organized decision-making group that must solve the firm's internal problems to develop a working team. It is believed such behavioralistic aspects are essential for a meaningful gaming experience.

[1] The traffic industry includes consumer products one can carry from the store, such as toasters and waffle irons.

The Spirit of the Marketing, Production, and Financial Aspects of the Model

The modeled market allows the managers of each firm to *create* and *implement* an economic marketing strategy such as low price, big volume, or high price, high markup. The strategy development consists in selecting the prime demand determinants to vary and the long-run method of changing them. The modeled market was developed to allow as wide a variety of feasible successful strategies as possible while, at the same time, requiring that each plan be based on a careful analysis of the total market. From HBS gaming experience it would seem that the three demand determinants of price, product quality, and marketing expense generate an interesting realistic market that allows a rich variety of strategies from nonprice competition to cutthroat pricing. Allowance was made for an intermittent factor of marketing expense, defined as promotion, to give a demand boost to a new product or a changed existing product. Included also was an allowance for the possibility of market research; for example, the purchase of information on potential markets. The research relationships were modeled to include a tradeoff between dollar budget and uncertainty of information. In keeping with the goal of economic strategy flexibility, the simulated market was formulated to grow as a function of the decisions of the firms and was not limited in total size or to a specific price pattern.

The production dimensions of the firm allow the managers to *control* the economics of a process. The control problem envisaged was one which required the coordination of all factors of production which could be readily represented in an economic fashion. The modeled process is a two-stage facility which requires inventories, labor, and fixed plant for each stage. All of the resources have different acquisition lead times. An interchange of labor between stages and products is allowed, but there are costs associated with this interchange. Fixed plant is variable in the long run, but a set amount of simulated elapsed time is required between the decision to expand plant capacity and the availability of this capacity for production. There are several response lags in the production system to changes in rate or mix which are represented as labor inefficiencies resulting in expenses. The simulation of production proceeds in twelve steps within the decision period of the firm to create a cumulative buildup or slowdown of the rate of output.

The financial character of the simulation provides the data creating a financial *planning* problem which requires the firm to relate internal requirements with a variety of external sources of funds. The internal cash requirement is created by significant fixed quarterly costs coupled with a highly seasonal market. The external choice problem is generated by allowing loans of varying simulated length each with a unique interest rate and requiring different financial conditions to qualify for each type of loan. In addition, each firm has the opportunity to sell more of its stock at an uncertain price. The stock price relates the total short-run and long-term profit activity of the firm thus providing the participants with a consistent measure of their own performance. To create a more realistic funds problem, the cash flow is calculated at twelve intervals during the decision period.

Experience with advanced executives and MBA students has indicated that a challenging gaming experience is developed in an expanding market with limited supply facilities. The challenge is to balance available supply with increasing demand. Thus, in the present model it is relatively easy to expand demand but difficult to take advantage of the expansion and achieve increased profits because of capacity restraints. In part, this approach is due to the nature of the simulation; it is solely an economic representation. In runs where demand has been curtailed and supply is in excess, it has been possible for responsible participant protest to identify forms of noneconomic marketing strategies, such as clever advertising or packaging, which might have allowed a firm to expand. A second reason for the excess demand is that it creates a more exciting game, which seems more fun for the participants as well as the Faculty. There are few losers.

The Structure of the Information

The game progresses at the rate of one simulated quarter of a year of economic activity for every decision set the firms submit.

Each firm having four or five students competes in an industry with four to seven identically characterized firms. On the basis of their experience in the simulation and their goals, the students create a set of decisions to control their firm. The impact of these decisions on the firm is obtained by manipulating the simulation model and the decisions of all firms in an industry. The result is industry sales by firm and the resulting profits of each firm. Exhibit 2 is an example of a completed decision sheet showing the dollar budgets. The present instructions to participants are reproduced in Appendix A. These instructions serve as an introduction to the simulation model and, with the output accounting statements, serve as a reference for preparing these budgets. The results of the simulation are produced as accounting statements, using common business terminology (see Exhibits 1, 4, and 5). The business context of the game provides a framework within which the players can organize their understanding of the instructions and the additional knowledge obtained during the experience of the game. The vocabulary of the reports is similar to the teaching material of the Harvard Business School MBA curriculum.

The amount of data in the accounting statement is intended to provide information that can be used with varying degrees of thoroughness. Each figure by itself represents the present state of the firm. Coupled with the same figure of the prior simulated quarter results, it may indicate a trend and, upon further analysis and experience in the simulation, the cause of the trend may be discerned. All the information is intended to be meaningful to the operation of the simulated firm. It is felt the quantity of data provides a rich enough search problem without the complexity of irrelevant information.

Industry information on competitors as seen in Exhibit 3 is the sort normally detected in the marketplace. As all the companies are considered publicly held, a profit and loss statement and the financial conditions of each firm in the industry are available each simulated quarter. Market information on competitors' activities is accurate for price, but only approximate for marketing expenditures, product quality, and sales volume. The figures on this latter information give the approximate level of expenditure or sales rate of a firm and identify large changes, but do hide small

EXHIBIT 2

Management Simulation—Decision Form

Industry 41 Firm 5 Period 6 Can Group 17

Purchase Plant $1000	Purchase Securities $1000	Dividends $1000	90-Day Loans $1000	One-Year Loan $1000	Five-Year Notes $1000		Sell Stock $1000			Ending Cash Position
200.	0.	0.	0.	500.	0.		0.		1	215,000
PRODUCT 1	//////////	//////////	//////////	//////////	//////////	//////////	//////////	//////////	///	////////
Price of Product $ per unit	Marketing Budget $1000	Promotion Budget $1000	Prod. Dev. Budget $1000	Mkt. Res. Budget $1000	MR- Price CPU	MR- Mkt. $1000	MR- Qual. CPU	MR- P.D. $1000		Forecast Orders
7.90	200.	0.	30.	0.	0	0	0	0	2	245,000
Raw Mat'l $ per unit	Fab. Production Rates Next Pd. 1000 units	This Pd. 1000 units	Fab. Labor $ per unit	Fab. # Men Assigned	# Men Hire (+) Fire (-)		Fab. Overtime # Hours			Finished Goods Production
1.10	260.	245.	1.00	260.	+ 10		0		3	245,000
Purchased Parts $ per unit	Asm. Production Rates Next Pd. 1000 units	This Pd. 1000 units	Asm. Labor $ per unit	Asm. # Men Assigned	# Men Hire (+) Fire (-)		Asm. Overtime # Hours			Product Profit (Loss)
.40	260.	245.	.70	182.	0		5000		4	400,000

PRODUCT 2										
Price of Product $ per unit	Marketing Budget $1000	Promotion Budget $1000	Prod. Dev. Budget $1000	Mkt. Res. Budget $1000	MR- Price CPU	MR- Mkt. $1000	MR- Qual. CPU	MR- P.D. $1000		Forecast Orders
3.30	200.	0.	30.	0.	0	0	0	0	5	65,000
Raw Mat'l $ per unit	Fab. Production Rates Next Pd. 1000 units	This Pd. 1000 units	Fab. Labor $ per unit	Fab. # Men Assigned	# Men Hire (+) Fire (-)		Fab. Overtime # Hours			Finished Goods Production
1.60	80.	65.	1.80	150.	+20		0		6	65,000
Purchased Parts $ per units	Asm. Production Rates Next Pd. 1000 units	This Pd. 1000 units	Asm. Labor $ per unit	Asm. # Men Assigned	# Men Hire (+) Fire (-)		Asm. Overtime # Hours			Product Profit (Loss)
.50	80.	65.	2.00	166.	0		0		7	100,000
PRODUCT 3										
Price of Product $ per unit	Marketing Budget $1000	Promotion Budget $1000	Prod. Dev. Budget $1000	Mkt. Res. Budget $1000	MR- Price CPU	MR- Mkt. $1000	MR- Qual. CPU	MR- P.D. $1000		Forecast Orders
0.	0.	0.	50.	90.	1800	300	900	0	8	—
Raw Mat'l $ per unit	Fab. Production Rates Next Pd. 1000 units	This Pd. 1000 units	Fab. Labor $ per unit	Fab. # Men Assigned	# Men Hire (+) Fire (-)		Fab. Overtime # Hours			Finished Goods Production
2.00	24.	0.	0.	0.	0		0		9	—
Purchased Parts $ per unit	Asm. Production Rates Next Pd. 1000 units	This Pd. 1000 units	Asm. Labor $ per unit	Asm. # Men Assigned	# Men Hire (+) Fire (-)		Asm. Overtime # Hours			Product Profit (Loss)
.55	24.	0.	0.	0.	0		0		10	-140,000

EXHIBIT 3

Industry Information on Competitors

```
                 I N D U S T R Y 41   P E R I O D  6

I N D U S T R Y  R E P O R T

F I R M   1        STOCK PRICE   9 1/4           DIVIDENDS PAID        0.
 PROFIT AND LOSS     FINANCIAL COND       INDIVIDUAL PRODUCTS
SALES RVNUE  2960.  CASH           132.  PRICE              16.15     7.00     0.
TOT EXPENSE  2567.  INVENTORY     1358.  MARKETING         152.28   302.08     0.
OPER PROFIT   393.  PLANT-EQUP    2568.  PROD DEVEL         18.87    62.10     0.
SECURTY INC     0.  TOT LIAB      1905.  DIRECT CPU          8.84     2.79     0.
NET EARNED    177.  COM EQUITY    3159.  SLS UNITS          39.97   331.12     0.

F I R M   2        STOCK PRICE   8 1/8           DIVIDENDS PAID        0.
 PROFIT AND LOSS     FINANCIAL COND       INDIVIDUAL PRODUCTS
SALES RVNUE  2999.  CASH           223.  PRICE               7.50    13.75     0.
TOT EXPENSE  2564.  INVENTORY      842.  MARKETING         365.48   150.52     0.
OPER PROFIT   435.  PLANT-EQUP    1927.  PROD DEVEL         62.66    24.42     0.
SECURTY INC     0.  TOT LIAB       555.  DIRECT CPU          3.58     6.53     0.
NET EARNED    209.  COM EQUITY    3457.  SLS UNITS         310.65    60.63     0.

F I R M   3        STOCK PRICE   9               DIVIDENDS PAID    50000.
 PROFIT AND LOSS     FINANCIAL COND       INDIVIDUAL PRODUCTS
SALES RVNUE  2806.  CASH           461.  PRICE               7.75    11.50     0.
TOT EXPENSE  2483.  INVENTORY     1193.  MARKETING         288.44   155.86     0.
OPER PROFIT   323.  PLANT-EQUP    1742.  PROD DEVEL         39.53    34.38     0.
SECURTY INC     0.  TOT LIAB      1223.  DIRECT CPU          3.29     5.39     0.
NET EARNED    151.  COM EQUITY    3128.  SLS UNITS         238.84    78.28     0.
```

F I R M 4		STOCK PRICE	5 7/8	CIVIDENDS PAID		22500.	
PROFIT AND LOSS		FINANCIAL COND		INDIVIDUAL PRODUCTS			
SALES RVNUE	2118.	CASH	439.	PRICE	9.10	14.00	0.
TOT EXPENSE	1996.	INVENTORY	1062.	MARKETING	270.54	124.34	0.
OPER PROFIT	122.	PLANT-EQUP	2081.	PROD DEVEL	57.31	23.44	0.
SECURTY INC	0.	TOT LIAB	1337.	DIRECT CPU	4.06	7.19	0.
NET EARNED	51.	COM EQUITY	2965.	SLS UNITS	156.71	46.05	0.

F I R M 5		STOCK PRICE	5 3/4	DIVIDENDS PAID		50000.	
PROFIT AND LOSS		FINANCIAL COND		INDIVIDUAL PRODUCTS			
SALES RVNUE	2767.	CASH	789.	PRICE	7.25	12.25	0.
TOT EXPENSE	2444.	INVENTORY	912.	MARKETING	314.80	211.70	0.
OPER PROFIT	324.	PLANT-EQUP	2010.	PROD DEVEL	32.84	29.40	0.
SECURTY INC	0.	TOT LIAB	974.	DIRECT CPU	3.29	5.56	0.
NET EARNED	149.	COM EQUITY	3678.	SLS UNITS	277.46	71.08	0.

changes. The rationale for this is that one can normally obtain the exact price of the competitors' product in the real world by shopping, but would only expect to know the general level of marketing by comparing competitors' activities with one's own. The purpose of this information on competitors is to make each firm aware of the economic activity of its industry to support the competitive interest in the game.

The Marketing Characteristics of the Simulation

The teaching objectives of the marketing characteristics of the simulation focus upon giving the student experience in developing and implementing the pricing and gross budgeting aspects of a marketing strategy. This experience is gained in an environment of a stylized traffic appliance market which responds to three known demand determinants. The total market is a function of the industry activity and will grow or diminish according to the appropriateness of the firms' decisions. An example of the economic diversity available in the model is a recent game which included two identical seven-firm industries with annual sales of $16 million at the start. At the conclusion of three simulated years of play, one industry had annual sales of $44 million and the other had sales of $18 million. The present total market has an adjustable secular growth, usually 4.5%. This total market is further modified by a seasonal factor intended to represent the quarterly sales pattern of the traffic appliance industry.

Each demand determinant of price, product quality, and marketing has a unique influence on the firm's market image. Price has the largest influence in the market and causes the quickest market reaction when changed. Product quality in conjunction with price identifies a product. The market reacts more slowly to changes in quality. Marketing budgets expand the demand for the products of a firm both in the quarter the money is budgeted and in succeeding quarters. Three forms of marketing budgets exist, and these are differentiated solely by their impact on the market. The budgets are called: (1) Marketing, (2) Promotion, and (3) Product Development. All budgets and price decisions must be considered in relation to the profit potential of the firm and the competitors' activities. The market and the available resources of each firm are such that a careful analysis of the market and internal resources should produce a strategy that guarantees a satisfactory profit. The key element to success is a planned sequence of decisions for molding a competitive plan. The simulated market responds to change more than to status quo and therefore maintaining all determinants constant does not often bring a reward of growth.

Identification of the specific product has purposely been left vague. The present simulation is not intended to be the exact replica of a given product market. To develop such a simulation for a competitive model would require an enormous research investment, and it is doubtful if the added verisimilitude would be worth the effort for our purposes. By emphasizing the planning aspects of the process and by omitting the identification of the product specifically, the participants are forced to scrutinize the data with fewer biases.

In order to introduce the game to students, the functions in the model have been created to simulate the responses at a gross level of the traffic appliance industry. Since it seems to help students to be able to think of a product at the start, the industry is introduced as similar to the traffic appliance market. As the students become involved, this aspect diminishes in importance, because they adjust to competing on pure economic terms. The present model seems to respond adequately as a traffic appliance market, there having been few complaints from over 6,000 students.

Generalization of a market without specifically defending it has been reasonably successful in preventing arguments from disgruntled individuals who feel the model does not react like the real market. There is no real market, and the participant needs only analytical and synthesizing ability to survive in the simulation. All have an equal opportunity to do well or poorly. This eliminates any library research and prevents a superfluous investment of outside time trying to see how or where the model does or does not relate to real life. There is a place for such activity, but not in a decision simulation game. Introducing too realistic a market or market description might shift the focus from the process of analyzing the market data to analysis of the simulation rules.

This would further emphasize winning and de-emphasize the learning experience of the student. The competitive environment of a Master's Program in Business Administration contributes more than enough to the winning phenomenon.

Definition of the Influence of Demand Determinants

The specific influence of a given determinant and the sequence of economic cycles are uniquely defined for each simulation by a series of parameters. These parameters can be modified from run to run as desired by the Faculty administrator responsible for organizing the game. This discussion of influence of determinants is general and indicates the intended response of the market to firms' decisions. Parameter changes modify total market size, the makeup of sectors of the market, rate of economic growth, seasonality, and the relative advantage of each firm. Allowing a firm a monopoly influence was found disruptive to this simulation and, therefore, all firms were kept equal in their effectiveness in the market. It is conceivable that qualitative factors in marketing, such as the nature of an advertising plan, could be accommodated by altering the marketing parameters of each firm.

Sales are generated in a series of sectors each of which considers all previous and present marketing decisions. It has proved useful to describe these sectors during the introduction session. They are not described in the Participant Instructions as the description would add too much detail. The spirit of the sectors can be communicated fairly quickly. The sectors are differentiated by initial relative size and particular response to the determinants. They were defined to represent five consumer groups typical of the traffic appliance market. The absolute size of each sector is influenced by the economic index and the seasonal factor. This combination of influences with the present parameters creates the following causal relationships:

(1) The market becomes more price sensitive in times of economic downturn.
(2) After three quarters of upturn the market becomes relatively price insensitive.
(3) The largest season is the third quarter and the lowest, the first.

(4) Similar prices and nonprice competition by marketing and quality will expand the market but not as much as price spread coupled with the identical nonprice competition.
(5) Sales level is dependent on prior sales level and present marketing activity.
(6) A firm's sales growth may be a result of growth of sales by the industry or acquisition of a competitor's potential sales depending upon its activity; e.g., quality improvement primarily hurts competitors, marketing budgets generate new demand, and price reduction creates new demand, thus robbing competitors in about equal proportions.
(7) A firm can create and maintain for itself a market if it maintains a majority of the demand determinants at that price-quality range in its favor; e.g., a product with a $20 price, $10 quality, and $80,000 marketing budget would hold its market share in competition with a product of $19 price, $9 quality, and a $50,000 marketing budget.
(8) Lost sales of a firm go to competitors.

The largest sector is most influenced by price and marketing budgets, assuming an acceptable quality ratio. It can be considered the large standard brand sector and is strongly affected by the economic index. The next largest sector is most influenced by the price to quality ratio, with an acceptable level of product development necessary. This sector can be considered the intelligent consumer market and is the most seasonally dependent, but it has the greatest long-term sales stability because it does not decay easily. The next three sectors are about the same size. One is influenced most by marketing and quality. This might be considered the private brand or local product market which has a very stable demand since the economic influence is slight and brand loyalty high. Another sector is the one that is influenced equally by quality and product development. It can be considered the style conscious high-priced product market and is fairly price insensitive but sensitive to the economic index. The final sector is influenced most by price. This is the price sensitive fad or style conscious market sector which has no stable demand because it responds to market activity.

The simulation calculates demand for a sector by combining demand determinants of each firm into an industry demand index, which includes past quarters' sales and the economic indices, and multiplying this index by past sales to generate total industry sales. The firms' sales are then calculated by creating indices for each firm, based on the firms' present and past marketing decisions. Shares of the industry sales are apportioned on the basis of the indices. Finally, the firms' sales are apportioned to the product on the basis of product indices. A weekly sales rate is then obtained; this rate has a constant growth or decay from the end of the prior quarter to the end of the present quarter.[2] To obtain sales, each product's weekly sales are then compared with available stock for each of the 12 simulated weeks. Lost sales are returned to sector demand as a residue of sales and parceled out again to similarly priced competitor products.

The Most Important Demand Determinant: Product Price

Price is the prime identifier of this traffic appliance market. As stated earlier, the profitable price range is from $4.00 to $44.00. Lower priced items tend to have higher sales volumes, but quantity expenses can make them less profitable than middle priced products. Beyond $44.00, the sales volume will not support the semifixed and fixed costs of the present simulation. The market sectors view the constellation of prices as defining the market, and a given product is identified by its general price range. The product number on the decision and accounting sheets has no identifying characteristics for the simulated market, but it is necessary for data processing. Competition is keenest between similarly priced products. There is relatively little competitive interaction between products differing widely in price. A firm with widely spread prices will generate more sales per marketing budget dollar than a firm with similarly priced products. Since the market sectors differ in their price sensitivity, an industry with a wide range of prices will have a larger total market than an industry with bunched prices. As an example, three products, each priced at $7.20, having about equal quality and marketing budgets would share a total dollar demand smaller than a similar set of products whose prices were $8.00, $7.20, and $6.50. The lowest priced

[2] A simulated quarter is defined as having 12 full weeks of economic activity.

product, other things being equal, would sell the largest volume.

How the Product Quality Image Is Determined

Product quality is determined by the amount budgeted per unit for labor and material in the simulated manufacturing process. The *labor quality index* for normal products is the sum of the straight time value of scheduled labor hours per product in the fabrication and assembly departments. The *material quality index* for normal products is the inventory value of the cost per unit of raw material, plus the cost per unit of purchased parts. There is an appropriate mix of ingredients for each total product cost. The quality indices for products whose ingredients are within 8% of the appropriate mix are equal to the sum of the dollar value of their inputs; for products whose inputs are not in balance within this mix, the cost of the unbalanced input is discounted in value to the median of the normal range of products. The following ingredient mixes for the total cost represent points on the geometric representation of appropriate mixes for this market. In essence this is the production function of the industry.

Costs of "Normal" Products

Fabrication Labor	$ .40	.75	1.05	1.40	2.40	3.60	4.50
Assembly Labor	.20	.40	.75	1.40	4.50	10.80	17.10
Raw Materials	.60	.85	1.10	1.35	2.20	3.40	4.50
Purchased Parts	.30	.35	.40	.45	.60	.80	1.00
Quality Total	$1.50	2.35	3.30	4.60	9.70	18.60	27.10

A product must have 60 cents worth of labor composed of 40 cents fabrication labor and 20 cents assembly labor, and at least 90 cents worth of materials, composed of 60 cents raw material and 30 cents purchased parts. For example, the firm with a product whose total cost is $6.00, with $1.00 assembly labor, 80 cents fabrication labor, $3.00 raw material, and $1.20 purchased parts would find the market discounting the abnormally high costs of raw material in line with labor to about $1.20 for raw materials and 50 cents for purchased parts, for a market quality image of

$3.50. The ratio of price to quality is a significant factor in calculating demand for similarly priced products. The market for high-priced products requires a lower quality ratio than the lower priced products, thus they have a higher markup.

Varying Time Impact of Marketing Budgets

Product demand is influenced by three types of marketing effort represented by budgets which are defined as promotion, marketing, and product development. They differ according to the time of their impact upon the market and their simulated time influence in the market. These three types of marketing are similar, since they tend to expand the demand for a product as well as the firm's sales. Each has a most effective range for a given level of sales; in other words, one has to spend a certain amount to obtain any influence and beyond a certain amount the added dollar does not return that amount of expenditure in profitable sales dollars. It is up to the participants to analyze the sales data to determine the limits and elasticity of the determinants.

The marketing budget represents the typical advertising expenditures a product would incur to influence the ultimate purchaser. These expenditures would include budgets for newspaper and radio advertising as well as normal selling expenses. As such, marketing is the most significant budget and typically will have the greatest influence of the three decisions. Sales reaction to a change in the budgetary level is most noticeable in the quarter the change occurs and in the quarter following. A marketing expenditure should be budgeted each quarter. Each expenditure has a discernible effect on product sales for about four quarters after it is made. The threshold of expenditure and maximum effective range are influenced by the price and unit volume of the product. For low-priced products, a minimum of $100,000 per quarter is necessary to have a significant effect. For products over $20.00 that have a sales volume of under 50,000 units, $100,000 is about the upper level of expenditure. This range is based on the reasoning that the lower volume high-priced products direct their consumer coverage to a specific audience and obtain better efficiency per marketing dollar. The reasonable range for all products is from about 30 cents per unit to $8.00 per unit of marketing budget.

Individual product expansion from marketing effort depends on its relative expenditure within the price range of its competitors. The sum total of all product marketing budgets in an industry can expand the potential market by as much as 100%.

Promotion expenditures have a greater impact and do not stimulate demand for as long a period as marketing budgets. They are included in the simulation to encourage the coordination of marketing moves. Expenditures should precede the introduction of a new product or significant change in an old one by at least one quarter. The purpose of the promotion budget is to fill the pipeline of distribution, and this budget represents selling effort to the wholesalers and dealers in the distribution system. This expenditure should precede all significant demand changes to obtain maximum benefit from the changes. It has a short-term effect since the marketing budget will support normal distribution expenses after a new or different product has been introduced. Product changes for which promotion expenditures would be appropriate would be a price cut of greater than 10%, a 33% increase in the product development expenditure, or an 8% rise in product quality. The effect of a well-timed promotion expenditure is a rapid market penetration or increased sales for an established product. A well-timed promotion budget will accelerate sales growth from 24% to 30%. Promotion budgets could typically range from 30% to 70% of the marketing budget.

Product development serves the function of styling and developing new products, improving the packaging of present products, and other normal long-term marketing expenditures. Changes in product development are noticeable two quarters after they have been made, and continue for eight quarters. They have a very long cumulative effect that is more significant in the medium and high-priced products than in the lower priced ones. The effective range of product development expenditures per unit sold for a $5.00 to $10.00 priced product is 15 cents to 45 cents; for a $10.00 to $20.00 priced product it is 30 cents to 90 cents; and for a $20.00 to $40.00 product it is 50 cents to $1.50. It is important to maintain this budget. A zero budget indicates the product is going to be discontinued, and sales are affected as the product development index becomes zero. Product development for one product does carry over for another in the same firm, with the result that product development expenditures, in some sense, can be considered to create brand preference. The specific effect of product development is the most difficult to identify, but past participants have done so especially in the higher priced products.

Market Research

Market research information is available to those firms that contemplate introducing a new product or modifying an existing one. The teaching objective is to give the participants a feel for the value of information and the problems associated with developing an experimental design. To obtain information, a firm must make a budgetary allotment to market research and define up to four demand determinants. The demand determinants are price, product quality, marketing, and product development. Because promotion budgets must be accompanied by a market change, it is impossible to obtain information on market behavior as influenced by this budget, and it is not an allowable dimension. Research for a new product must define at least price and one other determinant. The information obtained is the amount of sales the firm would have made had it sold the planned product during the quarter it requested the information.

There are threshold budgetary limits dependent upon the number of demand determinants to be investigated. Table I indicates the threshold budgets in effect.

TABLE I

Threshold Budgets of Market Research Expenditures

Number of Demand Determinants	*Market Research Budget*	
	Threshold	*Upper Limit*
One	$10	$50
Two	$30	$70
Three	$50	$90
Four	$70	$120

The levels seem to encourage students to use market research occasionally but not haphazardly. The accuracy of the market research report depends upon the budgeted amount. Below a defined threshold budget a firm obtains noise. In the first third of the effective range, a firm will obtain information that is within plus or minus 25% of the expected sales. In the middle third, the accuracy of the information is plus or minus 18%, and in the upper third the information is plus or minus 12%. Thus, a firm's marketing report can get as accurate as 12% of the real figure. The exact percentage is never known, since this is a random factor.

All research requests can obtain pure noise which is also a function of the budgetary amounts. The lowest range of market research budgets can expect on the average one time out of six to receive a false report. This report will not be identified, and it will be produced as if it were a real one. The middle range of budgets will provide noise once in nine times, and the upper level once every twelve requests. The market research phase is the only random element in the model and is an attempt to imitate the uncertainty of market research.

The market research demand figure is created by redoing the demand calculation of the normal simulation and substituting or adding, as the case may be, the new research determinants. The research report is produced at the bottom of the product report (see Exhibit 4). When obtaining market research information for a proposed product, using fewer than four variables, the value of the unspecified variables will be average figures for similar products in the industry. Likewise, when obtaining information for an existing product if fewer than four variables are changed, the values of the unspecified variables will be those actually used in the period in which the market research data were obtained. The resultant demand calculation is then made inaccurate in accordance with the level of the market research expenditure.

Competitive Aspects of the Model

The relative ranges described above are for the more typical simulations. The activities of the firms strongly influence the total market and the market will develop in accordance with these strategies. For example, if the firms all resort to price-cutting as the primary tactic with little nonprice competition, the market becomes very price sensitive and the low-priced market grows at

EXHIBIT 4

Product Income Statement

```
          I N D U S T R Y  41    F I R M   1    P R O D U C T   2

             I N C O M E   S T A T E M E N T    P E R I O D   6

REVENUE FROM SALES, AT $   7.00 PER UNIT                          $ 2323650.
COST OF GOODS SOLC AT STANDARD COST
   FABRICATION LABOR, AT $  0.90 PER UNIT         298755.
   ASSEMBLY LABOR,    AT $  0.60 PER UNIT         199170.
   RAW MATERIALS,     AT $  1.05 PER UNIT         350188.
   PURCHASED PARTS,   AT $  0.41 PER UNIT         135645.
   OVERTIME PREMIUM                                    0.             983758.
GROSS PROFIT                                                         1339892.

FACTORY OVERHEAD
   INDIRECT LABOR                                  34980.
   SUPERVISION                                    120624.
   MAINTENANCE                                    103008.
   DEPRECIATION                                    44704.             303316.

SELLING AND ADMINISTRATIVE EXPENSES
   MARKETING                                      325000.
   PROMOTION                                           0.
   COMMISSIONS AND SALESMENS EXPENSE              165682.
   WAREHOUSE AND SHIPPING                          60468.
```

PRODUCT DEVELOPMENT	60000.	
MARKET RESEARCH	0.	
ADMINISTRATIVE	74121.	685271.
OPERATING PROFIT		$ 351305.

P R O D U C T I O N

	FABRICATION DEPT.	ASSEMBLY DEPT.
PRODUCTION VOLUME, UNITS	422926.	414590.
W.I.P. INVENTORY, UNITS	106251.	70834.
NUMBER OF MEN HIRED OR FIRED	0.	0.
NUMBER OF MEN BUDGETED	430.	286.
NUMBER OF MEN WORKING	430.	286.
NUMBER OF HOURS AVAILABLE	212531.	142250.
PERCENT HOURS UTILIZED	98.	97.
NUMBER OF HOURS OVERTIME	0.	0.

I N V E N T O R I E S

RAW MATERIALS AT $ 1.10 PER UNIT, 102074. UNITS
PURCHASED PARTS AT $ 0.45 PER UNIT, 160410. UNITS
FABRICATED PARTS AT $ 2.00 AVERAGE PER UNIT 35417. UNITS
FINISHED GOODS, IN UNITS

BEGINNING		77319.
PRODUCTION		410422.
GOODS AVAILABLE		487741.
ORDERS RECEIVED	331950.	
SALES LOST	0.	
SALES VOLUME		331950.
ENDING, AT $ 2.97 AVERAGE COST PER UNIT		155791.
SHARE OF INDUSTRY UNIT SALES VOLUME, PERCENT		21.

the expense of the high-price market. In such a market a $4.00 product might be very profitable. Another market might expand by large marketing expenditures and quality improvements. This market would support several high-priced products with large margins and reduce the sales potential of cheap products. This is important to keep in mind for two reasons:

(1) Successful tactics in one simulation game are not transferable to subsequent gaming exercises, and students should be cautioned to ignore prior "good" strategies.
(2) Complaints about market idiosyncrasies can be related to the behavior of the firms in the industry.

The Production Aspects of the Simulation

The objective of the production phase of the management simulation game is to give the students an experience in controlling the economic functions of a two-stage process. The two-stage process affords an opportunity to cope with the full range of production problems, and ample data are provided for the implementation of a variety of analytical approaches. Production control problems include maintaining an appropriate balance of inventory for a seasonal demand, designing productive capacity by defining the proportion of resources, and developing routine decision-making procedures for dealing with uncertain demands with a process which includes several time lags. The production model of the simulation is completely deterministic and all direct costs are well defined in the instructions. How certain indirect costs are derived is completely defined for the firm but only partially revealed by the instructions to the participants. These costs are those typically unknown in a real firm and relate to how indirect labor costs fluctuate with an added volume of goods and how the overhead rates vary with different quantities of output. Experience with the firm allows the student to codify costs to some degree. All production costs are defined each quarter (see Exhibit 4).

Each firm can produce from one to three products with one production facility. The productive facilities available are composed of relatively fixed resources, referred to as plant and equipment, and variable resources, termed labor. Plant and equipment decisions deal with the long-range sales to capacity problem, and as such are designed to establish the absolute upper constraint on production capacity which has a slow rate of change. Fixed assets depreciate at a rate of 2½% per quarter and therefore, to maintain plant, an investment must be made equal to the amount of depreciation. To expand plant, additional investments equal to the size of the desired capacity must be made two quarters prior to the utilization of the desired expansion. Plant cannot be sold. Reduction in size is obtained by allowing depreciation to reduce the total value of the plant. There are automatic implementation costs associated with plant expansion which are related to the size of expansion. For minor expansions below 10% of the existing plant, the charge is about 8% of the new investment. For larger expansions, the surcharge percentage increases up to about 30% for a 100% expansion. These charges are to reflect the normal operating costs, during an expansion, and the expected side costs for the plant change. The increasing cost structure in addition to representing realistic contracting fees is intended to make large changes expensive and to reward the participants who achieve capacity expansion in a series of well-planned moves.

Production Capacity

The basic determinant of capacity is book value of plant and equipment. For each $2,500 worth of plant and equipment a firm may employ one unit of labor defined as a man. Additional men above the one man per $2,500 may be hired, but beyond the proportion of one man to $2,315 of plant there will be no output from increased hiring. This restriction represents the relation between fixed and variable resources and seems to provide an adequate rate of return on capital investment of up to 15%. Each man can produce $900 worth of product each simulated quarter at normal costs, and $225 worth of product at overtime rates. Labor is budgeted in hours at a charge of $1.80 per product per hour. Thus, each man can produce up to 500 hours of output at straight time and 125 hours of overtime per quarter. The firm must decide how much labor input per product is desired. The amount of labor per product determines the quality image of the product, and the number of men available establishes volume limits.

The labor for each product is assigned to one of two departments—either fabrication or assembly. The production process is serial in that each product must be processed first in the fabrication department and then the assembly department. There are inventories associated with each department which must be maintained at certain levels to produce at designated rates. Raw material inventory must be available for the fabrication department and work in process of fabricated parts and purchased parts must be available for the assembly department. To pose an interesting rate response problem, a production pipeline has been created by requiring three weeks for a product to be processed in the fabrication department and two weeks for a product to get through the assembly department.

Indirect Costs and Labor Inefficiencies

A firm producing three products will have three fabrication departments and three assembly departments. The management of the firm receives the product report as shown in the bottom half of Exhibit 4 and this defines for each department the number of men assigned, the level of inventories, and an efficiency factor identifying how well the firm utilized its labor the prior simulated quarter. This utilization is the determinant of the cost of changing the process. As such it represents the cost associated with transferring men to different departments, changing production rates in the department, and hiring new men to the department. The intent is to reproduce the normal inefficiencies of changing the production rates and plant capacity through variable costs which are related to the change.

Workers can be hired for a cost of $200 and a first quarter efficiency of 50%; they can be fired at a cost of $50. The cost parameters were developed to provide an even tradeoff for hiring a man prior to the availability of a new plant as against hiring a man during the acquisition period. If a man is hired prior to the expected plant capacity availability, the cost is 50% of usable labor wasted; if during the period new plant expansion is available, the cost is 50% of low plant capacity wasted. A worker is hired by a specific department but may be transferred to other departments in response to market shifts. Any transfer is allowable, but transfer between similar departments (fabrication of one product to fabrication of another) is most economical. The firms are informed of the transfer costs in the instructions. As noted above, these are accounted for during the simulation as labor inefficiencies. All transfers, at least cost, are made automatically by the simulation and require no decision from the participants. The inefficiency information is provided to allow accurate production output predictions.

For an established product, changes in production rate greater than 15% create additional inefficiences proportionate to the amount of change: a 25% change in rate level would reduce efficiency of a department for one quarter by 20%, a 50% change would reduce the efficiency by 40%. These costs are in keeping with observed work force behavior and emphasize the inherent costs of rebalancing lines for higher production rates and the like. The easiest method for short-term changes in the production rate is by use of overtime. Use of overtime incurs indirect expenses in addition to the normal hourly rate of $1.20 per hour for assembly labor and $1.80 per hour for fabrication labor. The cost differential normally makes overtime profitable in the assembly department and unprofitable in the fabrication department. All of the costs associated with changing production rates are not defined in the instructions, but experience with changing the production rate will allow the firm to define them. The marginal cost of adding plant versus working overtime favors overtime in the short run and adding plant in the long run. The emphasis of this phase of production is primarily focused on smoothing production by balancing capacity with an annual sales forecast.

An aspect of the production model which emphasizes future planning and seems realistic relates to acquisition of materials. To ensure adequate inventory, the planned production rate for each department for the present and the next quarter must be specified, thus at least a two-quarter forecast is required. Raw materials which are used in the fabrication department have a simulated 30-day lead time, and purchased parts for the assembly department require a 45-day simulated lead time. For normal production at least a 30-day inventory of raw materials and a 45-day inventory of purchased parts must be on hand at the end of one quarter for orderly production during the beginning of the next quarter. In order to maintain the appropriate inventory levels, parts are ordered automatically on a cost-per-unit basis by a simulated purchasing department.

The ordering rule is:

Raw Materials Order = (Production Rate This Period − Present Raw Materials Inventory) + ⅓ Production Rate Next Period

or

Purchased Parts Order = (Production Rate This Period − Present Purchased Parts Inventory) + ½ Production Rate Next Period

Inventories are drawn on a FIFO basis and valued as such. Carrying costs of 1½% per period of maximum inventory value are charged. These inventories do not suffer obsolescence or deterioration.

Calculation of Production Output

The following description is how the simulation model manipulates the decision inputs to produce a finished goods inventory. A skimming of the material can give the flavor of the process. This information is provided to afford the development of detailed game assignments. The balance between total number of men and book value of plant and equipment is evaluated first to insure that at least $2,315 of plant per man exists. If an excess of men exists, the productive potential of all newly hired excess men is first eliminated and then the excess is eliminated by reducing available manpower for each product in proportion to the percentage of the total number of men assigned to each product. Total productive labor time per week is then calculated for each department on the basis of the assigned men per department. The first four weeks have 41 hours per man and the last eight have 42 hours of time. Hiring and transfer inefficiencies are then subtracted for the appropriate weeks. Hired men work 0% the first week and 100% the last with a linear improvement during the 12 weeks. This calculation results in an available man-hour-per-week figure per department.

The desired production rate is then compared with the prior production rate. Production changes up to 12% are realized during the first week which has an output equal to the average of the old rate and the desired rate. Each additional 3% of change up to 21% takes an additional week to obtain the desired output. Changes of 22% to 50% take up to two months; volume changes of 50% to 100% take the entire quarter. A new product has zero output the first week and the desired rate of output, if resources are available, thereafter. (Note: A three-week delay exists to start assembly because of no in-process parts and the normal process delay of the fabrication department.) The analysis of rate changes by the simulation model produces a maximum allowable output per week per department due to production rate decisions. This maximum is compared week by week with available hours, the minimum constraint being the amount possible to produce. If the maximum allowed rate of production exceeds the available hours, and overtime hours are scheduled, overtime hours are assigned starting in the last week of the quarter up to the maximum allowed production rate and proceed week by week until all allowable overtime hours are scheduled. The result is available productive labor hours per week.

The final production constraint is that minimum material and work-in-process inventories must exist for the fabrication department and the assembly department to maintain a normal output. A five-day work-in-process inventory of fabricated parts must exist to obtain normal production in the assembly department. The simulation proceeds by multiplying the labor budget per product by the available productive hours to obtain the desired production rate per week; the fabrication output is obtained by selecting the minimum of available raw material or available productive labor hours. This minimum amount becomes the first week of the work-in-process of the fabrication department, and the prior third week of fabrication work-in-process is added to the work-in-process inventory between departments to compute the output of the fabrication department. The assembly production rate is determined by taking the minimum of the available purchased parts inventory, 60% of available work-in-process inventory, or available productive labor hours. This amount is then added to the assembly work-in-process, and the prior second week of assembly work-in-process is added to finished goods inventory. This process is repeated twelve times for each decision period. After the fourth cycle the raw materials purchased are added to the raw materials inventory, and after the sixth cycle the purchased parts inventory is augmented by the amount purchased.

The Finance Aspects

The principal objective of the finance sector of the simulation is to create a challenging financial problem which can be solved by balancing a number of relatively uncertain and interrelated factors over a period of time to achieve the firm's financial objectives. Some of the decisions the firm has to make, such as debt policy, dividend policy, and rate of asset expansion, are largely internal to the finance function itself. Others involve the interrelation between the finance function and the marketing and production functions. The role of the financial manager in the game is to advise his colleagues of the financial implications of decisions in all areas and to obtain for the firm the necessary funds in the most advantageous manner given a set of firm objectives.

Where all of these interrelated and interdependent decisions are tied together is in the stock market evaluation mechanism that has been developed for the simulation. The stock market price depends upon the amount of earnings per share, the history of earnings per share, the firm's overall rate of return on total assets, the dividend payout ratio, the recent pattern of dividend payments, the ratio of debt to total capitalization, and the current index of economic activity.

An example of how the market price generator has been designed to focus the students on the interrelation of the functional areas is as follows: It would be possible for a firm to have high aggregate profits and earnings per share as a result of effective marketing decisions and at the same time, because of greater working capital and plant requirements, to have lower rate of return on total assets than the second firm that has lower profits but a higher rate of return. The simulation model would give a higher stock market valuation to the second. Another example is that the firm could expand profitably with the result that both aggregate profits and rate of return of total assets would be higher than other firms and still have a lower market price than these other firms. This result might be obtained in two ways both suggesting that the firm grew too rapidly. First, it may have been necessary to sell additional common stock to finance expansion and thereby cause a dilution of investors' expected earnings per share, or the expansion may have been financed by what the market regards as reckless reliance on debt with the result that future earnings could be discounted at a higher rate to reflect the added financial risk associated with the enterprise. These examples have been given not to suggest that all firms accept the market evaluation as the only criterion of their performance, but rather to propose that the firms give the evaluation serious consideration. The suggestions have been made to provide the basis for a productive discussion about those firms that reject long-term market value as a primary measure of company performance. Such an interchange can focus upon the implications and consequences of such behavior to the firms' stockholders.

The decision role of the financial manager's job will be cash budgeting. Detailed budgets to explore the adequacy as well as the economical impact and the risks associated with alternative financing and operational plans should be developed. To date, various means of collecting payments as a tactical element of a market strategy have not been considered owing to the modeling complexity and the added requirement for the participants. The section below will begin with a discussion of how the cash requirements are simulated and will define what generates these requirements. The discussion will then describe alternative methods of obtaining funds and the probable implication for the firm.

Cash Requirements

The cash requirements and flow of funds are calculated in the simulation week by week throughout each 12-week simulated quarter. This calculation is made to reflect the normal turnover in a business and to pose a dynamic cash forecasting problem. Short-term loans are available on the first day of the quarter.

Requested loans are significantly cheaper than loans initiated by the bank to maintain the firm's cash position. If a firm estimates its cash position will fall below the required minimum of 5% of cash expenses, it is advantageous to request a 90-day loan.

Cash expenses fall into three general classes: (1) expenses which result from an explicit budget decision and are cash payments during the quarter; (2) implicit expenses which result from the normal operation of the firm and may or may not be defined in the instructions; and (3) explicit budgets for which payments are partially or completely deferred to a future quarter. The first class of expenses includes all labor payments, promotion budgets, product development budgets, market research budgets, dividends, and purchase of securities. The second class includes loan and interest payments, costs associated with changing capacity, and normal indirect expenses. Implicit expenses and their sources are defined in Table II.

TABLE II

Implicit Expenses of a Firm

Class of Expense	*Determinant of Amount*
Interest and Loan Payments *	Due Date and Amount of Loan
Contracting Cost for New Plant	Relative Size of Expansion
Indirect Labor Costs	Number of Labor Hours Scheduled and All Unused Labor
Factory Overhead	Size of Plant
Shipping Expense *	Unit Volume of Sales
Warehousing Expense *	Number of Units of Maximum Inventories
Hiring and Firing Costs *	Number of Employees Hired or Fired
General Administration *	Units of Production and Size of Plant
Selling and Administration *	Dollar Volume of Sales

* Explicitly defined in instructions.

The following expenses are deferred to next quarter: one-third of the amount of the purchase of raw materials, one-half of the amount of the purchase of purchased parts, up to one-third of the marketing budget to the next quarter, and the full amount of the purchase of plant and equipment.

Sales are considered to be made on a net 30-day payment contract. The expected value of accounts receivable is about 33% of sales. This varies as much as plus or minus 8% in a manner influenced by the state of the economy and the season. Accounts receivable tend to be a larger share of sales during the big selling season or economic downturns, while they tend to be a smaller share of sales following the high selling quarter or during economic upturn. This reflects the feeling that in a given concern receivables, while uncertain, quite often exhibit known general patterns.

Securities may be purchased or sold. They return a rate of 1% per quarter, starting the quarter after their purchase. There is a fee of 1/8 of 1% for purchasing and no fee for selling securities. Securities are available to afford the opportunity for utilizing idle funds. An explicit decision must be made to buy securities. Short-term loans at 3% cannot be held to purchase securities.

Sources of Available Funds

The several sources of available external funds include short-term unsecured loans, short-term secured loans, short-term emergency credits, medium-term loans, long-term bonds, and common stock. The short-term unsecured loan, medium-term loan, and long-term bonds will be available only to those firms that meet and continue to meet fairly demanding tests of financial conditions and earnings. The ratios on which these tests are based are printed on the balance sheet as shown in Exhibit 5. All tests are on a pro forma basis; in other words, the ratios are calculated by using numbers which are expected to appear on the balance sheet at the end of the quarter assuming the loan in question is granted. The interest rate on these funds will be less than from other sources. The repayment of loans granted to firms meeting these tests will be quickly accelerated if their financial position subsequently deteriorates. The most serious case of a deterioration of financial condition would force a company to sell common stock at depressed prices in order to refinance its called loans.

The simulation determines the financial conditions for loan requests at the end of the quarter with the loan included. If the firm

EXHIBIT 5

Balance Sheet and Cash Flow

I N D U S T R Y 41 F I R M 1

B A L A N C E S H E E T P E R I O D 6

CASH		131980.
SECURITIES		0.
ACCOUNTS RECEIVABLE		1006915.
INVENTORIES		
RAW MATERIALS	161773.	
PURCHASED PARTS	95518.	
WORK IN PROCESS	475264.	
FABRICATED PARTS	118685.	
FINISHED GOODS	506260.	1357500.
CURRENT ASSETS		2496395.
PLANT AND EQUIPMENT, NET		2568205.
T O T A L A S S E T S		5064600.
ACCOUNTS PAYABLE		360972.
NOTES PAYABLE		553061.
TAXES		191316.
CURRENT LIABILITIES		1105349.
LONG TERM DEBT		800000.
COMMON STOCK	500000. SHARES	2095000.
SURPLUS		1064251.
T O T A L L I A B I L I T I E S A N D E Q U I T Y		5064600.

```
TOTAL LIAB TO    LONG TERM DEBT     QUICK    CURRENT    FIXED CHARGES
TOTAL ASSETS     TO TOTAL ASSETS    RATIO     RATIO       COVERAGE
   37 0/0            16 0/0          1.03      2.26        12.44

STOCK PRICE $  9 1/4

          C A S H   F L O W
CASH SALES                                                              1953416.
CASH FROM ACCOUNTS RECEIVABLE                                            839693.
INCOME FROM SECURITIES                                                        0.
CASH FROM 90 DAY SECURED LOAN, ISSUED BEGINNING OF PERIOD               537516.
CASH FROM 90 DAY SECURED LOAN, ISSUED END OF PERIOD                      15545.

T O T A L   R E C E I P T S                                             3346170.

TOTAL CASH EXPENDITURES (INCL INTEREST)                                 2653091.
TAXES PAID                                                                    0.
SECURITIES PURCHASED                                                          0.
CAPITAL EXPENDITURES, PLANT                                              525000.
DIVIDENDS PAID                                                                0.
REPAYMENT OF 90 DAY LOANS                                                173353.
REPAYMENT OF ONE YEAR LOAN                                                    0.
REPAYMENT OF FIVE YEAR NOTE                                                   0.

T O T A L   D I S B U R S E M E N T S                                   3351444.

N E T   C A S H   I N F L O W                                             -5274.
```

meets all the requirements, the simulated cash flow is recorded; if it does not meet the required credit ratings, cash at higher interest is granted and the period resimulated with the additional funds necessary to maintain the required liquidity, which may be more or less than the requested loan. This in effect allows the bank a perfect information pro forma statement. The use of pro formas introduces a lag to represent the time lapse from submission for negotiation to receipt of the money and to require a careful analysis of financial requirements. The following explanation points out the requirements for loans as the simulation is now programmed. Simple parameter changes can be made to alter the specific values of the discriminating ratios.

1. *Short-term Unsecured Loans.* These take the form of 90-day notes with interest at an annual rate of 3% and available only when requested in advance. The simulation will not allow a firm to hold securities and an unsecured loan simultaneously. To be eligible for such a loan, a firm must meet the following requirements:

(a) Liquidity. A pro forma ratio of cash plus accounts receivable to current liabilities (including all loan payments due within one year) must be greater than 1.2 to 1.0.

(b) Profitability. Profits must have been earned in the previous quarter.

(c) Capitalization. A pro forma ratio of total debts, that is, the ratio of current liabilities plus short-term debts, plus longer term debt to total assets must be less than 30%.

(d) Borrowing History. A firm cannot have had 90-day unsecured loans for four consecutive periods.

2. *Short-term Secured Loans.* These cash loans are available in the form of 90-day loans bearing interest at an annual rate of 10%. Secured loans may be either planned or unplanned. This type of financing will be supplied automatically if planned financing is either inadequate to maintain the cash level or unavailable because more rigorous financial tests associated with preferred sources of credit cannot be met. To be eligible for a secured short-term loan a firm must meet the following requirement for collateral: a pro forma of short-term secured loans to finished goods inventory plus accounts receivable of no more than 80%.

3. *Short-term Emergency Loans.* This source of funds will be available when a firm cannot qualify for any other source of bor-

rowed funds. When such emergency funds are required, they will be made available in the form of 90-day notes bearing interest at an annual rate of 20%. Such funds will be provided automatically and therefore need not be ordered. Those companies forced to use emergency credit will encounter the following additional requirement for capitalization: no emergency loans will be approved for continuance if the pro forma of total debt (current liabilities plus short-term debt including emergency credits, plus longer term debt) to total assets is greater than 70%. In the event this overall capitalization ratio is exceeded, the company will be forced to sell common stock in the succeeding quarter to pay off outstanding loans at a presumably depressed price. A special loan is provided to meet contingencies in the interim period.

4. *Medium-term Loans.* One-year nonamortizing notes at an annual rate of 4½ % interest will be available only if ordered in advance. To be eligible for medium-term one-year notes a company must meet and continue to meet the following tests:

(a) Liquidity. A pro forma ratio of cash plus accounts receivable, plus securities to current liabilities, including loan maturities due within one year must be greater than 1.2 to 1.0.

(b) Profitability. Profits must have been earned in at least three of the four previous quarters.

5. *Long-term Bonds.* Five-year bonds will be available at an annual interest rate of 6%. For these bonds, there is an annual sinking fund requirement. The sinking fund requirement begins on the sixth quarter following issuance of the note and is at the rate of 1/20th of the original issue. In the second period following issuance of bonds, an amount equal to the quarterly sinking fund is included in current liabilities for pro forma analyses. The unpaid balance is paid in the twentieth quarter. Bonds are available only if ordered in advance. To be able to sell bonds the company must meet the following criteria:

(a) Fixed Charges Coverage. The average cash flow must exceed the fixed charges over the year ending with the current quarter. As computed by the following formula, the fixed charges coverage must be greater than one:

$$\frac{\text{Profit Before Taxes} + \text{Depreciation}}{\frac{\text{Sinking Fund}}{(1-\text{Tax Rate})} + \text{Interest}}$$

Interpretation: The profit before tax figure is an average of the current plus previous three quarter earnings before taxes; the depreciation figure is the current quarter's depreciation; the sinking fund figure is the current quarter's sinking fund plus the quarterly sinking fund if the note in question is issued; and the interest figure is the current quarter's interest plus the quarterly interest if the note is issued.

(b) Capitalization. Five-year notes may not exceed 30% total assets.

6. *Common Stock.* Each quarter a stock price will be generated for each firm. As noted above, the stock price is a function of the amount and pattern of earnings per share, for the most recent eight quarters, the firm's overall rate of return on total assets, the recent amount and pattern of dividend payout ratios, the ratio of debt to total capitalization, and finally the current index of economic activity. When a firm has a debt, with positive earnings for four quarters and paid dividends in the last four quarters, the stock price will rise. The rate of the rise is influenced by all factors. Companies can sell stock either voluntarily or, as outlined above, by being forced to sell as a result of emergency conditions. To sell stock on a planned basis the firm must specify the net dollar amount it wants to raise. The simulation then takes this figure and divides by the stock price as of the end of the quarter, in which period the decision to sell stock is made. This factor is further modified by a dilution factor discounting the price as much as 25% in situations where the number of shares outstanding increases beyond normally accepted bounds. This new discounted stock price then determines the total number of shares to be issued. Given the new number of shares to be issued, a new stock price is generated and the funds obtained from this sale are available to the firm on the last day of the quarter. Such funds cannot be used to purchase securities until the following quarter. This final stock price is published in the quarterly industry summary.

In the model, the corporate profits are taxed at the rate of 48% per quarter. Losses are accounted for during the period by deducting from the cash outflow 48% of the loss. A loss is carried forward in the form of cash credits from quarter to quarter. Credits are only allowed up to the amount of taxes paid in prior periods. This parameter can be changed and in recent times the tax rate has started at 52%, been reduced to 48%, and then to 44% during the simulation to afford some appreciation of the impact of a tax cut. The starting position of the firms is particularly sensitive to cash.

An adequate amount of cash must be provided to allow the firms some freedom in the first move or two, while the participants are still unfamiliar with specific responses of the simulation. Cash assets should not be so great that the individuals never have to concern themselves with financial problems; this would be unrealistic in most industrial environments. It is anticipated that the suggested starting cash positions available with the standard program will provide a good hedge against bankruptcy in move one or two yet yield a challenging financial problem.

Faculty Aids in the Model

At the conclusion of each simulated quarter, a Faculty report is generated to distill the critical information that an individual would need to know about each firm to observe the economic activity of an industry. Such a report has been found essential to keep the Faculty member involved and to help him stay abreast of activity in six or seven firms in an industry. The first part of this report is an unrandomized version of the industry report shown in Exhibit 3, and the report is provided to give the Faculty an overall feel of market development. In past sessions it has often been convenient for a secretary to plot price, gross profit, and sales from these charts to maintain some feeling of market trend. Plans are for the plotting process to be automated in the near future.

Exhibit 6 is the Faculty report given on each firm in an industry. This report covers all firms in an industry and allows a detailed analysis of the status of the firm. The report includes a complete balance sheet, cash flow statement, the financial information, the income statement of the last quarter, and the product report focusing on production. These five sections are explained briefly, as follows:

1. BALANCE SHEET. This section contains the firm's Balance Sheet at the end of the period. All figures are in thousands of dollars.
2. CASH FLOW STATEMENT. This section summarizes the firm's cash flows for the period. All figures are in thousands of dollars.
3. FINANCIAL INFORMATION. This section contains se-

EXHIBIT 6

HBS Faculty Report of Each Firm in an Industry

INDUSTRY 41 - PERIOD 8 - FACULTY REPORT

FIRM 5

BALANCE SHEET[a]

ASSETS		LIAB/N.W.	
CASH	312.	ACCT PAY	315.
SEC	0.	NOTES PAY	0.
ACCTS REC	989.	TAXES	160.
INVENTORY	804.	L.T. DEBT	0.
PLNT-EQUIP	2303.	EQUITY	3933.
TOTAL	4408.	TOTAL	4408.

CASH FLOW STATEMENT[b]

SOURCES		APPLICATIONS	
OPERATIONS	204.	OPERATIONS	0.
LOANS	0.	DIVIDENDS	0.
SALE STOCK	0.	PLANT PUR	100.
SALE BNDS	0.	LOAN REPAY	0.
CSH-SEC DEC.	0.	BOND RET	0.
		CSH-SEC INC.	104.
TOTAL	204.	TOTAL	204.

FINANCIAL INFORMATION[c]

EPS	0.22	STOCK PRICE	9 1/4	SHARES OUTSTANDING	660102.
CURRENT RATIO	4.43	QUICK RATIO	2.74	L.T. DEBT/TOT ASSETS 0/0	0.

INCOME STATEMENT[d]

SALES		2818.
LESS C.G.S.		1347.
GROSS PROFIT		1471.
EXPENSES		
FAC OHD	402.	
S AND A	760.	1162.
OPER PROF		308.
INT EXP		0.
SEC INC		0.
TAXES		160.
NET PROFIT		148.

PRODUCT LINE REPORT[e]

	1	2	3
PRICE	7.25	12.25	16.15
C.P.U.	3.48	5.91	9.20
SLS UNITS	278.	64.	1.
MARKETING	205.	120.	10.
PROD DEV	40.	40.	5.
OPER PROF	275.	109.	-75.
PROD VOL	278.	64.	1.
FGD INV	0.	0.	0.
NR MEN	688.	224.	56.
HRS OVTM	0.	0.	0.

[a] BALANCE SHEET (in thousands of dollars)

CASH—self-explanatory
SEC—Marketable Securities
ACCTS REC—Accounts Receivable
NOTES PAY—Notes Payable
TAXES—Accrued Tax Liability
L. T. DEBT—Long-Term Debt
EQUITY—self-explanatory

[b] CASH FLOW STATEMENT (in thousands of dollars)

OPERATIONS—Cash Sales + Collection of Accounts Receivable + MARKETABLE SECURITY INCOME—CASH EXPENSES—TAX PAYMENTS
LOANS—Cash received from Loans
SALE OF STOCK—Cash received from Sale of Stock
CSH–SEC DEC—Decrease in the total of CASH and MARKETABLE SECURITIES
DIVIDENDS—Cash dividend payments
PLANT–PUR—Purchases of plant and equipment
LOAN REPAY—Loan Repayments
BOND RET—Bond Retirement
CSH–SEC INC—Increase in the total of CASH and MARKETABLE SECURITIES

[c] FINANCIAL INFORMATION

EPS—Earnings per share during most recent period
STOCK PRICE—Stock price at end of most recent period
SHARES OUTSTANDING—Shares of stock outstanding at the end of most recent period
CURRENT RATIO—$\dfrac{\text{Current Assets}}{\text{Current Liabilities}}$
QUICK RATIO—$\dfrac{\text{Cash + Marketable Securities + Accounts Receivable}}{\text{Current Liabilities}}$
L.T. DEBT/TOT ASSETS 0/0—Ratio of five-year Notes to total Assets

[d] INCOME STATEMENT (in thousands of dollars)

SALES—Total Sales
C.G.S.—Cost of Goods Sold
FAC OHD—Factory Overhead Expenses
S AND A—Selling and Administrative Expenses
OPER PROF—Operating Profit
INT EXP—Interest Expense
SEC INC—Income from Marketable Securities
TAXES—self-explanatory
NET PROFIT—self-explanatory

[e] PRODUCT LINE REPORT

PRICE—Product's unit selling price
C.P.U.—Product's manufacturing cost per unit
SLS UNITS—Number of units of product sold
MARKETING—Total marketing expense incurred for the product (figures in 1,000's)
OPER PROF—Product's Operating Profit in 1,000's
PROD VOL—Product's unit production volume in 1,000's
FGD INV—Product's unit Finished Goods Inventory in 1,000's
NR MEN—Total Number of Men in fabrication and assembly departments assigned to the product
HRS OVTM—Total number of hours overtime (figures in 1,000's) budgeted for the product in both departments
0/0 UTIL—An indicator of the efficiency of the labor force in both of the product's manufacturing departments

lected financial ratios and statistics pertinent to the firm's operations.

4. INCOME STATEMENT. This section contains the firm's Income Statement. All figures are in thousands of dollars.

5. PRODUCT LINE REPORT. This section summarizes information pertinent to each of the firm's Product Lines.

A supporting publication for the Faculty is a detailed flow diagram of the model. This is only of interest to individuals who want to understand exactly how the model works.[3]

Concluding Remarks on the Model

The model will probably be modified continually in some small detail for better adaptation to the environment and the changing teaching goals of HBS's educational programs. This model is felt at present to represent a good balance of complexity, realism, requirement of student and Faculty time, and it seems to accomplish several teaching objectives of a professional business school curriculum. It should be pointed out that experience in dealing with the simulation of an economic activity has modified the original tactics of gaming, but the comment applied to war games still holds, namely, there is a continual balance between simplicity to allow the students to focus on the decision-making process and realism to make this decision making a more vivid experience. To achieve this balance is an art of design.

The present model has proved itself by preventing bizarre strategies. It does encourage consistent planning and decision making. It does not involve much noneconomic creativity, since this is not its function. The main purpose of the simulation is to allow the individuals to develop a rational economic strategy and to attempt to implement this strategy in a realistic environment. The details included in this model have been chosen for pertinence to the teaching goals, not primarily for reality. The amount of realism included is to provide descriptive background to the simulated environment in order that participants can experiment with the forms of analysis

[3] A copy of the flow diagram and documentation can be obtained by writing to the Division of Research, Harvard Business School, Boston, Massachusetts 02163.

and synthesis appropriate for an MBA curriculum. This token realism is an attempt to provide an experience in the essence of decision making without the needless complexity of mazes and dead ends. With this in mind, the model is designed for a minimum of Faculty assistance in explaining the operation of the game and a maximum opportunity for counseling the firms and judging their performance. On the basis of the last four years' experience, it would appear that the simulation does involve the individuals satisfactorily and enables the Faculty to function as counselors and clinical observers of the firms' activities.

CHAPTER IV

Game Design

Chapter II developed the theme that game development is an iterative process of selecting learning goals, defining organization, and creating pedagogic designs. These results are modified as more experience is obtained and better solutions for attaining the teaching goals discerned. A pattern of planned change seems reasonably successful in accomplishing a continuous improvement of a game and in maintaining the interest of the faculty. Immediately upon conclusion of a game session, students and faculty are polled for an appraisal of the experience to generate desirable modifications to the model and instructions. After modifications in the model are made and new instructions prepared, it is desirable to have a trial run of the game to introduce the new simulation to the faculty and test out new procedures. Assignments are then developed to complement the model and moves are scheduled to define the game. The following description of the functions necessary to carry out such a program includes a discussion of typical student response and feasible written assignments.

Faculty Game Activities

The teaching objectives of this game represent the intent of a heterogeneous faculty concerned with preparing a professional manager in a graduate school. The specific objectives change from year to year but the general spirit is to design a laboratory experience in decision making which would complement an MBA curriculum.

The functions necessary to create a decision laboratory can be classified as follows:

(1) Developing the game.
(2) Operating the simulation.
(3) Introducing the rules.
(4) Arbitrating student suits.
(5) Overseeing firm performance.
(6) Counseling firm members.

The development of a game must first define how the participants should operate within the simulated environment. This includes: (1) specifying the amount of student time the game will absorb; (2) defining the faculty roles; (3) sequencing the simulation decision periods, class discussions, and written assignments; and (4) arranging to insure that the necessary logistics are satisfactory. Often a committee of interested, informed members from a variety of subject interests can generate a balanced program taking advantage of the varied teaching opportunities of simulation gaming. The committee can serve as a very useful sounding board for new ideas during the planning stage, as a receptive body to suggestions during the gaming session, and as an informed decision-making group for developing an improved game. A game administrator, normally a member of the faculty, should be responsible for insuring that all the details of the simulation model are in order and that the game is conducted in a timely and effective manner.

The operation of the simulation requires an individual responsible for making all the data processing as error free as possible. The data processing for the present simulation consists in collecting the decision forms, keypunching the decisions into cards, running the simulation on the computer, printing the results in the desired number of copies, and returning the results to the appropriate students and faculty. Data processing procedures have been developed on the premise that little or no human interaction on the part of the students or the faculty is very desirable. Thus, the computation procedures have been developed in a way that simulation sessions can be conducted without requiring any simulation model revision or computer expertise on the part of the faculty or the students. The data processing responsibilities are normally given to a research assistant. The game administrator works with this individual in checking out the simulation to insure it is working correctly, to prepare the histories for dissemination to the students at the start, to set up the procedures for collecting the decision sheets, and so forth. This checking function includes creating interesting starting points for each firm to provide a challenge for the students but to prevent their going bankrupt very fast. In essence, the game administrator controls the information flow between the simulated firm and its student managers.

It is very desirable to differentiate the role of the individual who makes the introduction and performs the explanation from that of the faculty member who serves as a board of director member or counselor and staff aide. When a few well-informed individuals introduce the rules, the students consider them as the model experts. The students then refer to these individuals when a question arises on the rules or model functioning. This reduces the faculty need for expertise on the model and even more importantly it focuses the students' discussions with the boards and counselors on their decision problems instead of on what is wrong with the simulation.

A necessary element in most games is to have some individual to whom the students can turn when they have made an error or misinterpreted the rules, or when a data processing error has occurred in the simulation process. Typically the game administrator serves as the rule arbiter. The participants will occasionally shift a decimal point or inadvertently forget a calculation. The initial shock and the resultant chaos in the firm communicate to the students the importance of planned human redundancy when dealing with a computer. Since the effects are often cumulative and are artificial in their impact, redress is desirable in cases where other firms would not be influenced by changing the history of the firm. If the error does influence the other firms and would require a resimulation of the quarter, no change is made but often some cash rebate can be provided to the individual firm.

The role most vital to the teaching objectives of the game is that of an overseer to whom each firm must account for its own performance in the simulated industry. This function is best performed by two or three faculty members serving as a board of directors to a group of firms. To achieve a variety of backgrounds and interests, a multiman board seems desirable. The purpose of this group is to encourage the members of each firm to conduct the firm's affairs in a responsible managerial fashion. A faculty board which maintains an active interest in the activities and performance of a firm typically obtains a desirable level of rational analysis and conscientious planning from the students in carrying out their duties with the simulated firm. The general duties of this board consist of being informed on the decision-making activities of their firms and querying the students during the process of play on the rationale of their decisions. The board conducts the concluding session and performs the necessary grading.

Stimulating students to experiment with analytical tools, to question their decision-making processes, and to observe their reactions to their associates during the exercise is vital to the pedagogic success of gaming but difficult to attain. One of the most promising approaches is to establish a hierarchy in the student organization and to encourage the student leaders to demand reports and follow up on them. The student reports can then be made the subject of class discussion or serve as reports to a board. Another common method has been for the instructors, as a part of the normal classroom activity, to suggest a specific analytical approach for a class of game problems, give an example of how this approach might be used, and give an assignment to evaluate its use in the game. An alternative method of using analytical tools is to give a specific written assignment to each firm listing several pertinent techniques and asking the firm to utilize at least two and report back their results.

Guides to Game Development

In developing a game it is very desirable to establish a set of policies to guide the committee and administrator. Often these policies are not defined explicitly but expressed as the desire of the faculty. In considering the recent experience in gaming, the following policies were useful in guiding the game development:

(1) The simulation session is to be a coordinated effort of all required first-year MBA courses.
(2) It is to complement the present program and as such is to be considered as a laboratory course.

(3) A maximum of four hours per week of student preparation time per move is desirable.
(4) The total elapsed time should not exceed eight weeks.
(5) Board of director faculty time should be no more than a half-hour to an hour per move to keep informed of the activity of his industry.
(6) Pre-simulation session game time of the faculty should be kept to a minimum.
(7) The organization of the simulation participants should be such that it would encourage discussion and interchange of information among the firms.
(8) All teaching assignments and written requirements should be defined prior to the game session.
(9) A significant amount of effort should be allocated to aiding the students in assimilating the rules and getting into the process of play as managers of a simulated firm as quickly as possible.

Design Decisions in Developing a Complementary Game

To obtain maximum learning potential a game should generate problems relevant to classroom activities and maintain its momentum as a competitive exercise. Operationally how a game is implemented in a teaching program is a function of how many quarters of simulated activity are scheduled and the elapsed period of time the game will continue. Once the number of moves and the time span of the game are established, the timing of the decisions, the method of introduction, and the concluding session have to be scheduled in such a manner to avoid disrupting other classes and to allow adequate game preparation time. The most direct ties to the curriculum are the written assignments and discussions which should be tailored to the subject matter of the courses.

The teaching objectives seem best attained for the bulk of an MBA class in about 12 quarters of simulated activity. A few firms reach a plateau of understanding after eight or ten moves and some are just beginning to have a glimmer at twelve, but the majority of students are operating well in the twelfth move. Experiments indicate that an elapsed time of four to six weeks of decision making and a follow-up week for writing and the concluding session are most satisfactory with the present simulation model and set of assignments. During this period the interest and enthusiasm of the students in carrying out their firm activities are sustained, and adequate time is available to complete and discuss the written assignments.

An important aspect of a game is the organizational structure of the students into industries and firms. Experience has indicated that the present simulation works best with four or five individuals per firm. Three seem too few and the men get overworked; there does not seem to be enough work for six students. When in doubt it seems best to err in the direction of overwork, as idle participants get bored and can disrupt the simulation. The simulation model responds best as a game with from five to eight firms in an industry, although it can adequately handle from three to ninety-nine. Below five, one firm has too significant an influence, and beyond eight, the particular effect of one firm is very slow to be detected and each firm's market shares are fairly stable.

The method of faculty organization is an unresolvable issue. When the board supervises a set of firms from different industries, all firms to a board can be given an identical starting position. Early discussions on specific problems of adjustment and goal setting are relatively easy to generate because firms are eager to acquire insights and will talk with noncompetitors. Discussions near the end are difficult to develop, since most industries are very dissimilar with the firms having few common problems. A board with competing firms is a bit incongruous and poses an impossible situation for developing general discussions early in the game because firms are unwilling to disclose their plans to their competitors. The concluding sessions are very lively since firms' false impressions of competitors can normally stimulate a fruitful discussion on proper bases for decision making. This form of supervision is more work for each faculty member, however, since he must stay informed on several different firms from the start.

Pre-Game Session Activities

Pre-session activities unique to gaming and contributing significantly to the game success are complete pre-test of the game, involvement of the faculty in making a few moves, creating interesting firm starting positions, and the understandability of written instructions. The adequacy of written instructions to the participants is critical to a smooth start. Not only should they be written to be assimilated fairly readily, they should also be organized to serve as reference. The instructions in Appendix A have been through seven revisions and seem to define without ambiguity how to operate in the simulated environment for the stated teaching objectives. If the objectives change, the instructions should change also.

The simulation model should be tested by running it for at least four more quarters than the game run is scheduled. During this run a variety of unusual decisions should be made to test the model thoroughly. The test sessions are opportune for allowing the faculty to become more familiar with the simulation game.

It is important to give the faculty a feel for the dynamics of the game data in preparation for serving as a board member. An adequate familiarity can be obtained by scheduling the faculty to test segments of the simulation and by maintaining the remainder of the decisions constant. For example, the production and financial decisions are left constant and the test firm varies the marketing decisions to evaluate the marketing constraints. Such procedure allows the faculty to become informed about how the model functions and the format of the information, without becoming too involved in the competitive aspects. As for changes in a tested model, experience shows that it is easier to live with a minor discrepancy than to try to correct the computer program after a game has started.

Developing the appropriate histories for starting positions of the firm is a time-consuming effort but is quite important for a useful concluding session. If one firm feels it had a poor position or another a favored position, its managerial effort in the game can be dampened and nonfunctional discussions can be generated. The goal is to have each firm a bit different but to have equal market opportunities. To introduce the rules, at one time a set of histories was created to include identical prices and resources for all firms, basing the instruction exhibits on these data. Each firm, then, was allowed to observe the reaction of the market and the production system to its own decisions and to compare these with what other firms achieved. This introduction also made the question period after the practice session more meaningful to all firms, since the details of the production decisions and the financial decisions were based on identical accounting statements and related to the instructions. However, the method proved too artificial and created more problems than the similarity of data solved.

In recent games the firms have been given the practice move in the identical position they will assume at the start of the game. Quicker introductions to the market have resulted. Because of the seasonal cycle, the firms are provided with four quarters of history of their firm for the practice move; this system is applicable to their actual simulation run. It is important to include in each firm's four-quarter history as many significant changes in the simulated environment as possible to aid the student in observing feasible responses. For example, the history should include a new product introduction, a large loan, and a price reduction. These data allow the firms to observe seasonality, repayment of loans, and the influence of plant and equipment changes.

Observations on Student Reaction: Folklore of Gaming

Using a game for teaching purposes requires faith that the student will profit from the entire process. To the instructor first using a game, the initial student reaction is disturbing, and this response can raise grave doubts about having started the process. Aggressive student response can induce an apologetic attitude from the faculty to the participants: "I'm sorry I got you into this mess, but it's only a game and we will be through soon." This attitude is harmful to the learning potential of the simulation game because it encourages the participants to play the role of gamesters and not economic decision makers. The faculty should play its role as a board of directors and conscientiously require each firm to develop and to implement a business strategy. In order to provide some basis for this faith, four common phases of behavior that students exhibit in a simulation game are presented. Student responses which will be discussed are those of the typical successful student group that manages to attain some working relationship, becomes involved in the simulation, and fulfills its goals in the game—the most common game experience for typical MBA students.

The introductory phase, when the students are learning the rules and are becoming acclimated to the simulation data, is marked with a great deal of individual floundering and student anxiety. This anxiety generates long discussions with the game administrators and faculty on how unrealistically the simulation functions, thus preventing them from operating effectively; or how immensely sophisticated the model seems to be with complex rules far beyond them, thus accountable for their poor results. The second general phase is one wherein the students suddenly seem to understand the rules and accept them as the reality within which they must function. Comprehension seems to stimulate a great deal of analytical activity and long discussions between firm members concerning the validity of their predictions. In the third phase the group begins to develop plans independently, to make adequate analyses which are coordinated, and to develop a feasible strategy. The final stage is carrying out the plan they have developed and improving their strategy. It seems that this is an important culmination to the gaming activity, and time should be allocated for the firms to observe the results of their efforts.

The introductory phase can be aided by a careful explanation of the rules, by allowing the students adequate time for preparation of the practice move, and by an exhaustive discussion of the practice results. However, it is impossible to involve all the participants, and some will not understand the gaming environment. The faculty can assist these individuals by urging them to stop creating hypotheses about how life differs from the simulated environment and by suggesting they buckle down to dealing with the available information and work within that framework as realistically as possible. During this time it is important to stress that the model is not meant to represent life but a distillation of experience about how some markets behave and some manufacturing systems function. For emphasis, the data have proved meaningful to several hundred students who have made analyses in a businesslike manner and developed appropriate strategies. The introductory phase, even with the practice move, somehow seems to take at last two simulated moves of the firm in their industry for the majority of students to operate effectively. Allowing more practice moves does not seem to reduce the number of learning moves in the game.

Once the students are involved and understand how to operate in the simulation, they tend to spend too much time in detailed analysis of all the available data without any attempt at discriminating what is important to their firm. At this phase of the game it is opportune to require each firm to define its goals and policies for submission to the board of directors and for the board to require its firm to defend the bases they are using in order to plan for the attainment of these goals. It is very helpful to have small discussion groups including several noncompeting firms start an exchange of ideas on appropriate methods of analyses. Moves three through five seem to be one of the more critical phases of the simulation. If the firms do not understand how to operate in the environment or cannot achieve a working group because of personality problems, it is essential to provide faculty assistance.

Following the great bulge of analytical work, the students develop confidence in their ability to make decisions concerning the simulated firm and will produce decent predictions. At this time they begin to have a little more fun with the simulation and become a bit too involved in implementing a market strategy. The firms understand how to provide enough product to meet market changes, how to obtain the financial resources for various tactics and are aware of their competitors' activities. In this phase it is desirable to present some case analyses or class discussions on issues related to the game, such as:

(1) The influence of the information format on the organization.
(2) The effect of various marketing forecasting techniques.
(3) How one determines product profitability within a firm.

The competitive aspects are intense at this time, and game discussions seem to reduce some of the emphasis on winning and to focus on the process of decision making.

The final two or three moves allow the completion of most firms' plans, and the results are an evaluation of how well the firms handled the data. The students spend at most an hour to an hour-and-a-half per move on these last few moves, since their prior decisions have set the stage for what is going to obtain. However, the final written assignment normally stimulates reflective discussions on the firms' performance during these moves and this is valuable to the learning experience of the game. Given three full years of simulated activity, which is the amount found most desirable, the members of the firm should have had an opportunity to develop their own strategy and demonstrate to themselves that it will work. This confidence often stimulates lively discussions in the concluding session on how each firm perceived its opponents' activities and how these differed from what the opponents thought they were doing.

Gaming in a business school curriculum does create one form of student behavior that is not too desirable—overenthusiasm. A few individuals often not doing well in the curriculum become quite involved in the game and spend too much time in analysis and developing firm decisions. Because they do spend the time they become experts on the industry and become leaders in their firms. This can cause the entire firm to spend too much time on the game and ignore other courses. A timely word can at times prevent such occurrences.

Course Game Assignments

An important aspect of the design of a simulation game is the development of course assignments relating to the simulation material. A significant problem in developing the course assignments is the timing of the subject matter as it relates to the game and the course. From the game point of view it would seem all assignments should come early in the game so that participants can obtain some experience from the results of their discussion. However, in addition to the constraint of time, the participants' lack of experience with the simulation makes early discussions superficial. A feasible method is to have written course assignments after move two or three and then ask the students to submit a written summary of their analyses of specific problems such as sales forecasting or source of funds, four moves later when appropriate for the course. A second approach is to hold discussions on problems of simulated firms from a prior game run. Using the problem data creates a common data base for class discussion which does not relate to a particular strategy of any firm but is in a familiar format and is pertinent to the game and course activities. It is important to make the data of all outside material relate to the same hypothetical firm thereby eliminating the drudgery of reanalyzing pages of accounting information.

The simulation data have been designed to pose a rich variety of problems in the control, finance, marketing, and production areas. All aspects of the simulated firm have to be solved for successful operation in the simulated environment and thus are dealt with whether assigned or not. The assignments are intended to focus upon a particular decision in order to encourage the use of the substantive material in the normal course work to solve the problem. The assignments discussed below have been utilized in the Harvard Business School MBA game as links to the courses. However, the game material can be overworked to the extent that it becomes a bore for the students with the result that one of the prime reasons for using gaming is nullified.

Pertinent Game-Written Assignments

As noted in Chapter III, the simulated market has been developed to allow the development of a market strategy which is very dependent upon the firm's pricing policies. One assignment that stimulates a good bit of student reflection is to require a written statement identifying the bases for the firm's pricing policy at the end of one year of play. As their policy changes are successful because of market developments, the written comments can provide a good basis for the board to discuss the rationale of the firm's marketing policy.

Sales forecasting is an essential aspect of the simulation and has proved to be a very successful subject for an assignment. Requiring the students to create an explicit statement of their forecasting model at move four and requiring each firm to state the results of its forecast with each decision sheet have induced better forecasting in the game and have improved awareness among students of the potential and problems of forecasting. The forecasting assignment can be followed by a short case of a hypothetical firm considering what form of forecasting is best. An example of such a case would be a description of a firm that had projected future sales solely on the basis of historical trends and then considered shifting to an economic model for forecasting. The students rely on their game experience to evaluate the alternative and use class discussion to formulate a critical analysis of forecasting techniques.

The principal objective of the finance sector of the game model is to place the participants in a position where they have to balance a number of uncertain and interrelated factors over an extended simulated time to achieve a set of financial objectives. Where all the interrelated and interdependent decisions have been tied together is in the stock market valuation mechanism for the simulation. The market price of each firm's common stock will reach its highest level when the overall position of the firm relates most favorably to the valuation criteria that have been built into the model. As discussed elsewhere, these criteria include a variety of financial implications, and the balance of these factors escalates the stock price. Requiring each firm to submit a statement of its plans for borrowing money early in the simulation defines its financial intent. A follow-up assignment can then be given requiring each firm to defend its financial transactions and how they relate to possible stock market evaluation of the firm's activities.

Requiring cash flow forecasts throughout the game can influence the firm to focus on indirect expense procedures. Making the cash flow forecasts requires a detailed understanding of the indirect cost allocation in the simulated firm and this knowledge can generate a discussion on methods of allocating overhead. This discussion can be followed by suggesting a variety of methods of costing to evaluate how each method influences profitability.

The production aspects of the simulation have been designed to create a macro-production scheduling problem. All costs exist for making a tradeoff between capital expansion to acquire overcapacity or to level production by building inventories. Each individual firm must select an appropriate capital base and work force plus inventories to meet the seasonal demands of the market. An interesting assignment is one that requires each firm to define its production scheduling rule and to relate this rule to the goals of the firm. This assignment can emphasize the importance of forecasting and investment considerations of production planning procedures. In order to follow up on this assignment after the sixth move, each firm should predict its ending inventory position to evaluate the effectiveness of its rule. Such an assignment may encourage the firms to appraise the tradeoffs in production scheduling carefully and may persuade them to attain some experience in codifying a decision procedure.

Conclusion

Management game designers must carefully and completely develop the details of the simulation game prior to starting the exercise. Developing an interesting and challenging management problem to reap the rewards of a dynamic pre-coded simulation is not too different from other curriculum developments. The payoff is an exciting useful learning experience, resulting from the continuous prompt feedback to the student of the effect of his decisions. The prime cost seems to be loss of flexibility. Once started, the ingredients of the game are fixed and students and faculty alike are participants in observing the unfolding of the simulation. The sequential and accumulative nature of the process makes it very difficult to correct an oversight or remedy poor execution. Furthermore, as the activities involve competition between student groups, relatively minor errors in the model or assignments are magnified by the intensity of the involvement. In seven years of gaming, an error-free game has never been produced in spite of many man years of effort prior to the start. However, all the errors have been minor and have caused little disenchantment with the game. Thus the simulation is considered a fair and effective evaluator of a business decision maker.

CHAPTER V

Recent Gaming Experience

Now that the ingredients of gaming have been discussed, it seems appropriate to describe a few recent examples of the product of the gaming effort. The examples discussed are intended to provide the reader with a few alternative plans for utilizing the HBS model, and to add to his insight of what is involved in a business simulation game. During the past two years, the game utilized in the first year of the MBA Program at the Harvard Business School has been organized in two quite distinct fashions. The 1965 game was the best session held involving individual five-man firms and three-man Faculty boards directing an industry. This session is discussed to provide an example of the best effort with this design. A research experiment was conducted in conjunction with the 1965 game which in addition to the changes in the overall curriculum design called for significant changes in the design of the 1966 game. The 1966 game also discussed below improved the organizational behavior aspects and opened up new opportunities for further developments. The new design is discussed to describe an alternative method of implementing a game. This is followed by a description of the use of this model in an Advanced Management curriculum and as part of a two-week course.

Description of the Spring 1965 HBS–MBA Management Game

The 1965 HBS game was developed as a laboratory course in the first-year required MBA curriculum with the aforesaid teaching objectives of integrating functional courses and providing experience in decision making in a dynamic environment. The first-year MBA class of 670 students was organized into 21 industries of 7 firms each. The logistics for such a large class are not trivial, but the essence of the game session is identical to one game for 20 men in one industry. In conjunction with the game play an experiment on decision making and game behavior was planned. The results of the experiment are discussed in Chapter VI.

The game administrator, with the assistance of six other Faculty members, introduced the game to the students. The administrator was the sole arbiter of all procedural problems of the game and all simulation questions were referred to him. Each industry reported to a three-man board of directors assigned to evaluate the firm's performance in the simulation. The game started the first week after the students returned from spring vacation and continued for six weeks, concluding in the first week in May. Exhibit 7 is the schedule of the spring session.

EXHIBIT 7

1965 HBS Management Simulation Schedule

Date	Time	Event
Friday, March 19—		The Firm Assignments, Participant Instructions, Simulation Schedule, and Four Quarters of Firm History Distributed.
Monday, March 29—	1:10 P.M.	Section Faculty Introductory Class
	2:00–5:00 P.M.	Student Practice Decision
Tuesday, March 30—	3:00 P.M.	Results of Practice Decision Returned with the Written Assignments for the Simulation Session.
Wednesday, March 31—	3:45–4:30 P.M.	Discussion of Practice Run Results
Friday, April 2—	1:00–2:00 P.M.	Industry Meetings with Boards of Directors
	5:00 P.M.	First Decision Due
Monday, April 5—	1:10 P.M.	First Decision Results Returned
	5:00 P.M.	Second Decision Due
Tuesday, April 6—	1:10 P.M.	Second Decision Results Returned
	5:00 P.M.	Third Decision Due Together with Statement of Firm Goals and Policies

Thursday, April 8—	1:10 P.M.	Third Decision Results Returned
	1:10–5:00 P.M.	Boards of Directors Meetings with Individual Firms
	5:00 P.M.	Fourth Decision Due
Friday, April 9—	2:30 P.M.	Fourth Decision Results Returned
Monday, April 12—	8:30 A.M.	Fifth Decision Due
	1:10–2:00 P.M.	Case Discussion on "Small Group Behavior at HBS"
	2:00 P.M.	Fifth Decision Results Returned
	5:00 P.M.	Sixth Decision Due
Tuesday, April 13—	3:00 P.M.	Sixth Decision Results Returned
Monday, April 19—	8:30 A.M.	Seventh Decision Due
	1:10–2:00 P.M.	Case Discussion on "Technical Note on Moving Averages and Exponential Smoothing" and "Firm 7 Industry 19"
	2:00 P.M.	Seventh Decision Results Returned
	4:30 P.M.	Eighth Decision Due
Tuesday, April 20—	3:00 P.M.	Eighth Decision Results Returned
Monday, April 26—	8:30 A.M.	Ninth Decision Due
	1:10–2:00 P.M.	Case Discussion on Financial Planning
	2:00 P.M.	Ninth Decision Results Returned
	4:30 P.M.	Tenth Decision Due
Tuesday, April 27—	3:00 P.M.	Tenth Decision Results Returned
Monday, May 3	8:30 A.M.	Eleventh Decision Due
	2:00 P.M.	Eleventh Decision Results Returned
	4:30 P.M.	Twelfth Decision Due
Tuesday, May 4	3:00 P.M.	Twelfth Decision Results Returned
Saturday, May 8	5:00 P.M.	Final Report to Boards of Directors Due
Friday, May 14	1:10–2:30 P.M.	Industry Meeting with Boards of Directors

A practice move was scheduled for Monday after a 40-minute introductory class in which the objectives of the game were discussed, the role of the students defined, and the rules explained. Most of this class time was devoted to completing a decision set with reference to the appropriate page in the instructions and to the position of the data on the accounting statements. The students had been given the Participant Instructions and their firm assignments ten days prior to this meeting. Each firm had a four-quarter history of their firm. The 40-minute introductory session concluded at 1:50 P.M., and a practice decision set was required of each firm at 5:00 P.M. that day. The results of this decision set were returned after scheduled classes the next afternoon.

On the following afternoon, Tuesday, a question period on the results of the practice move was conducted by the individuals who introduced the rules. In preparation for these sessions the instructors checked the practice decision sheets and reports to note the common mistakes, such as lack of decimal points and improper number of digits. Unusual decisions were questioned in the class by the instructor to probe the firm's understanding of the rules. The period was spent in identifying the mistakes and answering questions on the rules, and concluded with a general discussion of the simulation procedures.

On Friday, following the practice discussion, each industry met with its board of directors. Each board gave its firms written assignments discussing them with the firms to encourage a conscientious managerial decision-making approach by the students in managing their simulated firm. If there were simple rule questions, these were answered, but the board referred most rule questions to the game arbiter. The intent of this meeting was to establish some rapport between the board and the individual firms and generate in the firms a feeling of responsibility to the board. The meeting de-emphasized the rules of the simulation and focused on the behavior of the individuals as managers of their firm. The remainder of the afternoon the students made their first decisions for their simulated firm.

The intent of the schedule was to have a series of moves close together to aid the students in learning the rules and becoming acclimated to the simulated environment. Scheduling the afternoon class as a game class and returning the results at the start of the scheduled time seemed to limit game activities to the afternoon with a minimum of interference from other class preparations.

With the third move the men submitted the goals the firm had developed, the policies they expected to follow, and the organization they had formed to carry out these policies. The fourth move was made two days later. The boards of directors met individually with each firm, during the afternoon scheduled for the fourth move, to discuss with them the appropriateness of their goals and policies and to observe how the firms were carrying out the simulation activities. Thereafter, one or two members of the board met with each firm at lunch to discuss their progress in the simulation.

A written assignment was given to each individual on Tuesday of the first week to present a plan for introducing a new product in a simulated industry. The material used for this written analysis was a case on a firm from last year's simulation game and included four quarters of industry sales data. The purpose of using a case was to provide a common basis for grading and to supplement the game data. This written analysis was due at 5:00 P.M. on Saturday of the first week. The purpose of the written analysis was twofold: (1) to make the individuals completely familiar with the data and functioning of the simulation; and (2) to encourage a careful analysis of product introduction problems in order to produce good new products in the game industries. The written assignment successfully achieved both goals and contributed to an improved game. To support this assignment, no new product introduction was allowed until after move four.

The game then proceeded at the rate of two moves per week for four more weeks. Each week the class would meet at 1:00 P.M. for a discussion on a game case, after which the results of the morning move would be returned to the students and they would have from 2:00 to 5:00 P.M. to make the second decision of the day. The results for this move would be returned the following afternoon and a decision would be due the following Monday at 8:30 A.M.

In addition to the occasional discussion of game activities which were pertinent to course material, scheduled discussions were held on cases of hypothetical simulated firms. The case discussions as noted were conducted on the decision day. The three topics included were:

(1) The influence of organizational structure on firm performance.
(2) Sales forecasting.
(3) Long-range financial planning.

Each case with about four pages of text identified how the management of the simulated firms saw the problem and what the proposed solutions were. This introduction was followed by from six to twelve pages of exhibits which were distilled data of a firm in a prior year's game that apparently posed the problem. The data presented were adequate for resolving the problem posed although there was no one answer because the answer depended on the goals the students selected.

The discussions on the cases provided support to the ongoing game activities. The great flaw was the variety of different environments. The first discussion was informative and meaningful, but the discussions became dull and superficial as the game progressed. A prime cause was that each case concerned a different firm with the result that the students analyzed their own data, four quarters of practice move data, and four quarters of distilled data for each of the four cases. In a recent game identical firm data were utilized for two cases with much better results.

At the conclusion of the twelfth move the men were given five days to prepare their final report and submit it to the board. The board then had six days to read the report in preparation for the concluding session.

The Faculty boards advised their firms in a variety of styles. Although all students were given a common written assignment, the concluding session depended upon how the boards related to their firms during the game. Some boards were very stern and demanded certain profit margins and earnings or they would call in the firm and demand an explanation, while others behaved more as counselors trying to point out various methods of analysis and suggesting procedures for experimentation. One board, as an example, defined its role as that of a judge interested in profits and nothing else, and graded accordingly. This board identified acceptable levels of earnings per share and the kind of dividend ratio they expected to see from their firms. The final session was a tense defense of each firm's activities.

Another quite imaginative board identified itself as a member of Kidder, Hornblower, Peirce & Witter, who had disposed of the prior managers of their firms. This board was giving the present firms a three-year lease to demonstrate their managerial potential, and the board expected the new firm not only to define new goals for the old lethargic companies, but to implement and achieve these goals. The final session was quite interesting to the board and firms both in discussing the appropriateness of the goals, given three years of experience, and in evaluating the effectiveness of implementation. Role playing by the boards is a desirable stimulant to conscientious decision-making activities and should be encouraged. See Chapter VI for a discussion on board influence.

The 1966 HBS Simulation Game

The intent of the 1966 game in addition to former objectives was to support the organizational behavior course experience in analysis of organizations by individuals within the organization. The game was scheduled for the spring term after all students had taken a course which involved a group of students working on a task and studying the behavior of the groups' decision making. The last part of this course was devoted to organizing the firms for the simulation.[1] This method of organization seemed consonant with the research findings on the 1965 game and formed a positive bridge to the organizational behavior curriculum. To provide an organizational challenge, six of the former "firms" were combined and relabeled "divisions" which reported to a top management group thus forming a corporation. Each division competed as independent firms with six similar divisions from other corporations. The model

[1] The method of organization was a class project and varied in a minor fashion from class to class. Typically, each ninety-man class divided itself into three groups of equal talent and interest. Each thirty-man group then selected a leader who in turn selected a staff and set of division presidents. The division presidents selected their division members with the assistance of the corporate staff.

was revised in a minor fashion to consolidate all external funds flow at the corporate level and each division was required to obtain its funds from the corporation. The basic marketing and production aspects of the model remained, as discussed in Chapter III.

The schedule shown in Exhibit 8 was developed by the Faculty who were assigned teaching responsibility for the game. One Faculty member was assigned to each class of ninety which was organized into three corporations. The hierarchical student organization allowed the Faculty member to function as a board chairman dealing with three presidents and their staffs. A general outline of activities was developed by the teaching group to concentrate game activities in the last part of each week. These activities included long-range plans from the corporations, proposals for capital budgets from the divisions, and discussion with specialist groups drawn from each of the divisions. For example, a discussion was held on forecasting with the marketing specialists and production managers.

The method of organization and the schedule proved very effective in developing a significantly improved learning environment. Concentrating game activities in one section of unscheduled time reduced friction with the curriculum and gave the students adequate freedom to perform the necessary game activities. Giving the students responsibility for overseeing profit-making aspects of the division and requiring them to defend the actions of their divisions generated a very effective simulation gaming organization. The student presidents seemed to play their role to the hilt and were able to stimulate their divisions to perform a great amount of careful analysis in order to create appropriate plans. The chairman of the board by requiring one report from the corporation initiated a series of analyses and forecasts from the divisions to support the corporate report. The corporate staff in attempting to sustain their position became quite active in leading discussions with division personnel on forecasting techniques, cash flow planning and production scheduling methods. The concluding sessions were quite lively as they focused on the substantive issues of control methods for decentralized corporations and the organizational impact of a staff.

There were some problems. The student hierarchical structure accentuated personality clashes and allowed overzealous gamesters to demand of their colleagues reports which required hours of

EXHIBIT 8

1966 HBS Management Simulation Schedule

April 6 Wednesday	2:40–3:30 P.M.	Introductory Class on the Simulation
	3:30 P.M.	Four Quarters of Firm History Distributed
	3:30–7:00 P.M.	Student Practice Decision
April 7 Thursday	8:30 A.M.	Practice Move—Results Returned
	9:00–9:30 A.M.	Discussion of Practice Move
	9:30–11:30 A.M.	First Decision
	3:30 P.M.	First Decision Results Returned
	3:30–7:00 P.M.	Second Decision
April 8 Friday	8:30 A.M.	Second Decision Results Returned
	8:30–12:00 P.M.	Third Decision
April 14 Thursday	2:30 P.M.	Third Decision Results Returned
	2:30–6:00 P.M.	Preparation of Fourth Decision
April 15 Friday	8:30 A.M.	Fourth Decision Results Returned
	8:30–11:30 A.M.	Preparation of Fifth Decision
	3:30 P.M.	Fifth Decision Results Returned
	3:30–6:00 P.M.	Preparation of Sixth Decision
April 21 Thursday	2:30 P.M.	Sixth Decision Results Returned
	2:30–6:00 P.M.	Seventh Decision Prepared
April 22 Friday	8:30 A.M.	Seventh Decision Results Returned
	8:30–11:00 A.M.	Preparation of Eighth Decision
	3:00 P.M.	Eighth Decision Results Returned
	3:00–5:30 P.M.	Preparation of Ninth Decision
April 28 Thursday	2:30 P.M.	Ninth Decision Results Returned
	2:30–5:30 P.M.	Preparation of Tenth Decision
April 29 Friday	8:30 A.M.	Tenth Decision Results Returned
	8:30–11:00 A.M.	Eleventh Decision Prepared
	3:00 P.M.	Eleventh Decision Results Returned
	3:00–5:30 P.M.	Twelfth Decision Due
May 2 Monday	2:30 P.M.	Twelfth Decision Returned
May 7 Saturday	5:00 P.M.	MSS Report Due
May 9 Monday	1:10–2:30 P.M. 2:40–3:40 P.M. 3:50–4:50 P.M.	Concluding Session

analysis and the generation of useless statistical inferences. This led to a few personality differences with resultant morale problems. The more typical outcome of the personality clash was the withdrawal from the simulation activities of one of the individuals involved. An unsolved problem is how to funnel the loser back into the game and create some process of transfer of managers.

The main suggestions for next year are to give the top managers and their staffs an opportunity to make a series of division decisions in order to understand the rules better. In addition, more time is desired between the practice move and the submission of the first move for the development of a corporation organization. The most important change is to make the game one of the projects the organization behavior course will study.

The Use of the HBS Simulation in an Advanced Management Program Session

The use of gaming in the MBA Program has generated the interest of business educators in other educational programs. An absolute adoption of a given game is not recommended, but adapting a model is suggested as an economical method of initiating gaming. The following alternative methods of gaming are discussed to demonstrate alternative uses for the present HBS model. These examples of how a given model can be adapted for different educational programs rely heavily on adequate Faculty support in the new environment.

The HBS simulation game has been used in an Advanced Management Program since the fall of 1964 to provide experienced management students with the opportunity to create and implement a strategy in a dynamic environment. The model posed a realistic challenge allowing these advanced students to experience the problems of economic strategy development in two years of simulated time. Thus, this game emphasizes the strategy development aspects of the game, and de-emphasizes the analytical decision-making aspects. The game was designed to focus upon a careful development of a strategy and its implementation with no assignments on the methodology of planning. To accommodate this approach the market was modified to be a little more explosive, and cash requirements were not as stringent as in the MBA game. The session is always scheduled to take place over a three-week period to allow a quick development of a total strategy and to allow its prompt implementation.

Different problems exist when introducing a game to experienced executives instead of to MBAs. The Advanced Management men have not been accustomed to performing detailed analyses and a few have successful habits of approaching their business problems which are not appropriate in the simulated firm. Thus, more attention must be given to how one analyzes the data to support a decision. This is particularly important in the production and cash flow aspects of the present simulation. To provide such assistance on an individual firm basis, each firm is assigned a staff assistant who has had previous game experience with the model. They are the staff assistants to the firm for only the practice move, and serve as aides to help the executives become familiar with the rules and the methods of calculation. A second tool of support is to provide flow charts (see Exhibit 9 and Appendix B) which define the analytical steps in the calculation of the production decisions and cash flow forecast.

The Advanced Management students are organized into five firm industries. Each firm is composed of four men with different functional experience. Experience to date indicates it is not desirable to allow an experienced executive to assume his normal functional role in the simulated firm; for example, sales managers cannot be marketing managers but must take production or finance. This form of organization creates a number of identical industries with firms of similar starting positions. One method is to have these identical firms discuss their strategies and results with a two-man board of directors during the simulation. By having similar firms, the directors can discuss the influence of a different strategy with the firms. Recently each industry has reported to one member of the Faculty.

In an executive group a good deal of care must be taken to demonstrate how the simulation relates to the curriculum. Prior to the game introduction a discussion is held on the process of economic strategy development and implementation as it relates to the simulation game. This discussion is integrated in the group's Business Policy course which uses the concept of strategy as defined in

EXHIBIT 9

Flow Diagram of Production Process

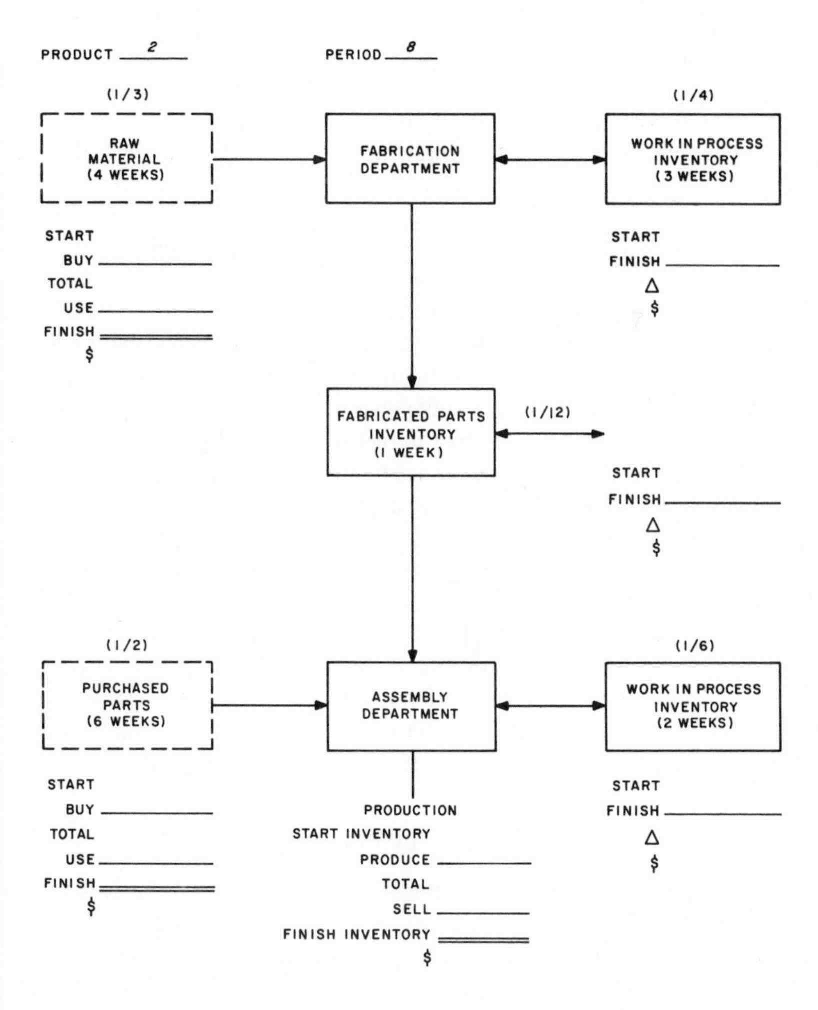

Learned's (and others) recent text on Business Policy.[2] The game is introduced by the Policy instructor and the game administrator. The instructor re-emphasizes the purpose and introduces a protocol of decision making he has found useful in playing the game. After he has demonstrated his procedures, particularly how he forecasts, the administrator discusses the rules of production and finance. The men then return to their dormitory rooms for their practice move assisted by a staff assistant.

The results of the practice move are returned the following day, and a discussion held on the results of this move. Thereafter the men make four moves in one week. Each firm is allowed four hours to make the analysis for each move. During this period the firms develop the strategy they intend to implement. After the third move each firm submits a statement defining its strategy in economic terms. A meeting is held with each firm and its two-man board to discuss the strategy and its implications. As noted above, the board meets with firms having identical resources thus providing the board with a good comparative basis for questioning each firm and developing useful discussion issues for the final session. For the remaining four moves each firm is allowed only two hours to make the analysis for each move, since by this time the firms are familiar with the simulation and with the process of implementing their strategy.

The final session is held with the firms that started in identical positions to discuss the evolution of firm behavior as a function of the various goals and policies adopted by the firms. This session includes problems of strategy development, and an overall appraisal of the various strategies based on the information available.

A Company Program

A second use of the HBS simulation has been as the basis for a Business Policy course in a company's two-week management development program.[3] Again the game was used as a means of involving the participants in the development of a business strategy.

[2] E. P. Learned et al., *Business Policy,* pp. 18–31.

[3] W. A. Bachman, "Sun Oil Establishes a Management School," pp. 70–72.

The purpose of this involvement was to identify the elements of strategy development, to demonstrate the interrelationship of functions in the firm, and to emphasize the importance of long-range plans. The program was conducted by the management development personnel of the company in conjunction with four consultants from universities. It was held at a hotel away from the common place of business with 28 of the firm's managers. The purpose of the total program was to develop in the managers an awareness of recent developments in management and imbue in them a professional sense of responsibility for their own growth. There were four main aspects of the program: (1) the business environment—economic and institutional elements; (2) decision processes—analytical techniques; (3) the human factors in the industrial organization; and (4) the simulation game—an exercise in strategy development.

The function of the game was to serve as an impersonal common problem on which the participants could test some of the concepts to which they were being exposed and then experiment in the development of a strategy. By carrying out this experimentation in the setting of a total firm, the group leading the program could develop an appreciation for the overall problems of strategy development needed to reduce the functional parochialism that existed in the company.

The two-week schedule allowed for one practice session and eight moves. A game administrator (teacher) introduced the game and discussed the problems of strategy development as they related to the simulation. Six firms of four or five men were formed with heterogeneous company responsibilities but each firm had members of similar status within the hierarchy of the management. The members of the firms were encouraged to specialize in jobs dissimilar to their own function. Each firm had an individual Faculty advisor who was to act both as a group counselor to introduce the procedures of the simulation as quickly as possible, and to aid the participants in using the materials they had been exposed to in their classes.

The game began on a Monday with an introduction which focused on the strategy development problems of the simulation and a minor discussion of the rules. Each firm then went to its firm conference room with its Faculty advisor who discussed the rules in detail and answered questions on the procedures. A practice decision set was due at 5:00 P.M. that afternoon. After dinner the results of the practice set were returned and a discussion held on the errors in a general meeting. The firms then started at about 8:00 P.M. to make the first move which was due at 11:00 P.M. that evening. The intent of the compressed two-decision format was to concentrate entirely on learning the rules for operating the simulated firm. Thereafter the firms were to concentrate on the problems of developing and implementing a strategy. A move was scheduled for each of the next three afternoons, and each firm was charged to develop an appropriate strategy and to submit this strategy with the third decision set.

Before the practice move, a detailed assignment was given to each participant to aid him in his role in the exercise. The assignment briefly defined the characteristics of the concept of a business strategy and gave an example of a concise strategy definition.[4] The general rules for the simulation were spelled out and the teaching objectives defined. To assist the men in developing their strategy, a set of feasible goals, appropriate policies, and typical organizations were included in the assignment. These goals and policies were intended to be examples of pertinent goals and policies for the simulated firm, and they were developed so a firm could not adopt all of them since they were mutually inconsistent. During the first two moves the firms were counseled to test various goals, to develop an agreeable set for their firm, and to formulate a consistent policy to achieve these goals. During the third move the game administrator discussed with each firm the appropriateness of its goals and implications of the policies selected.

At the beginning of the afternoon of the fourth move a general discussion was held outlining the necessary plans to implement a strategy in the simulated industry. Thereafter the advisors discussed planning approaches and the use of analytical techniques with the game data. A two-day break was followed by four moves with decreasing time allowed for each move. The second set of moves concentrated on implementing each firm's strategy. During these moves the Faculty encouraged the use of analytical techniques such as

[4] E. P. Learned et al., *Problems of General Management*, p. 88.

exponential forecasting and break-even analysis. After the concluding move each firm submitted a statement on the success of its strategy implementation and prepared an analysis of one of its competitors including a statement of its strategy. The last discussion was based upon these documents and the economic activity of the industry during the eight moves. The concluding session was informal and a bit on the humorous side to emphasize the learning aspects and de-emphasize who won. The important class discussion was on the problems of implementation after the strategies were defined. A final general session seemed desirable to allow the firms to conclude their experience and relate how they solved their problems.

One aspect of this game was a continuous informal discussion on industrial experimentation in decision making. The Faculty felt that these managers could improve the awareness of their experimentation capacity in the game. The men were encouraged to experiment with small budget changes to improve their understanding of the simulated environment thereby creating an experience base in the simulation. Rather than bring this industrial experimentation up in the game sessions it was discussed in the human factors session and in informal talks with the firms throughout the two weeks. This method of gaming seemed to provoke some insight among participants about how they were acquiring experience in the simulation and generated some very interesting discussions on the methods managers use to acquire experience. This point seemed to be a most interesting topic and was discussed at length in the concluding session.

The problems in dealing with a small group from one firm are probably obvious to most individuals engaged in management development. Familiarity with one's associates and status problems cause the firm organization issue to be significant. It is important to plan harmonious firms carefully to ease the human element as much as possible. The small number of students and intense Faculty support combined to obtain a productive use of the game in a short period of time. The economic activity of the game firms developed a basis for a comparative discussion on how their company differed from the simulated industry and posed several interesting issues on financial policies, employment practices, and marketing goals. The game in this environment served very successfully in providing a common vocabulary and set of problems for a group of executives in the same company who had been separated geographically and functionally for up to 20 years. By encouraging the participants not to choose their own specialty, but to assume a different function in the game, some understanding for the other manager's job was established. The personnel from the company felt this a significant asset of the game. In addition it provided a common experience for the men to talk on decision processes and strategy development as they saw them apart from their company. They could then relate this experience conveniently to their own company without political overtones. This background seemed to allow a discussion of problems in their industry and their company without reference or concern to the responsible individuals present.

Experience with this simulation in a short course is limited to five occasions. In such a course it is important that the majority of the teaching Faculty be very familiar with the simulation rules and economic model in order to take advantage of the relevant data. The firms served as the discussion groups for the human factor part and the game data were utilized as a basis for the analytical tools course. This game was developed jointly by the consultants and the company personnel for a series of two-week short courses. On the second trial, when the Faculty was familiar with the environment, adequate learning potential from the simulation was attained as an integrating factor and as a basis of discussion in the courses and informally on a range of problems. Such discussions proved the game's worth. However, to use a complex game as a separate course in a two-week program without an integrative effort seems an inordinate investment of time in gaming and is not recommended.

Concluding Remarks

In discussing the use of models, the need has been emphasized for adequate preparation and well-planned Faculty support of the gaming activity. As noted, this includes the clear definition of the role each Faculty member is expected to play and a general understanding by all concerned of the interrelationship of game and curriculum activities. It would seem that the single most important determinant of a successful game is Faculty involvement and intelligent counseling. Without these two ingredients, the game may be fun and absorb a good quantity of time, but will not be a worthwhile experience to the participants. The degree of involvement and counseling effort indicates how carefully the game is designed and planned, and how well this plan is understood by all involved in the gaming process.

CHAPTER VI

Gaming Research

A tradition of research on the use of gaming and on the decision-making behavior of the participants involved in the gaming process has developed concurrently with the development of management simulation games.[1] Gaming as a new approach to training decision makers required both evaluation and validation to secure its position in a curriculum. Most individuals developing games were experienced business researchers and naturally turned to producing research data to explore the learning potential of games. A well-developed game also afforded these researchers the necessary controlled environment for doing research on the business decision maker without interfering with a manager on the job or resorting to a sterile laboratory experiment. As has been discussed, for a game to be successful it must involve and motivate the participants to perform detailed analyses as a basis for their decisions. These decisions are normally intended to be as rational as any "real life" decisions and as such faithfully reproduce the decision-making process. Research with the HBS game has been of an exploratory nature since only evaluative issues have been considered. These experiences have been recorded to demonstrate feasible research activities.

Research on this and other simulation games has been performed

[1] For early overviews of the potential of management games, see Paul S. Greenlaw et al., *Business Simulation*; Cohen and Rhenman, "The Role of Management Games," pp. 131–166; W. R. Dill et al., *Conference on Business Games*; K. J. Cohen et al., *The Carnegie Tech Management Game*; Thorelli and Graves, *International Operations*.

to provide substantiation of the potential of simulation gaming as a means of training decision makers. It was a new technique viewed with skepticism concerning a simulation model's ability to convince and involve mature students. The main concern was that the artificiality of the simulation would reduce the learning potential of the game and that individuals would play it as a game giving little thought to the moves. Second, the simulation game was quite pervasive and influenced the complete curriculum; thus, it was not just one additional course or a new approach in a given course, but an adjunct that would affect all courses. In addition, the setup cost of programming and developing an appropriate simulation was on the order of tens of thousands of dollars and man years of faculty time. The purpose of the research was to achieve some data that would provide a basis for an investment decision possibly resulting in a significant change in the curriculum. The research for these data on the value of gaming has resulted in material suitable for comparison with other forms of management training, such as role playing or case studies. Faculty polls and participant questionnaires have been the main sources for evaluating the potential of games for business education.

Initial Game Experimentation at the Harvard Business School

The first two experiments with the HBS game were for evaluation purposes and have been published in greater detail elsewhere.[2] The second two experiments are noted in passing to give some idea of the available data that can be accumulated in a gaming environment. The most recent efforts are reported in some detail explaining how they relate to the methods of improving the gaming process and of investigating behavioral patterns within a gaming environment. The conclusions of the 1965 session sum up the present philosophy of gaming at HBS.

The First Evaluation Experiment

To obtain some data for appraising the value of gaming, an experiment was designed to measure the performance of the game

[2] J. L. McKenney, "An Evaluation of a Business Game"; J. L. McKenney, "An Evaluation of a Decision Simulation."

class and a class of students who were not involved in a game, and to compare these two types of students both before and after the game experience. An essay examination was given to two classes of ninety students at the beginning of the semester and at the end of the game. The students in the nongaming section prepared and discussed four integrated cases on production planning in lieu of the game activities. The test was to prepare an analysis of a business case similar to the ones that both classes discussed. The analysis was graded on three concepts of planning, defined as follows:

(1) Today's decisions create tomorrow's environment.
(2) Goals and plans are carried out by a series of consistent decisions that vary in accordance with the environment.
(3) Functional decisions of a firm are interrelated, for example, marketing decisions affect production and vice versa.

Grading was done by an independent grader with five years of experience in grading case analysis examinations; each paper was judged on a seven-point scale for each of the defined concepts. On the basis of a statistical analysis of the grading results, it appeared that participants in the game class were significantly better planners, as defined by concepts 2 and 3. There was no significant difference in grades for the first concept. The results gave some indication that gaming can help teach planning (as defined by the concepts) to decision makers. Nevertheless, the grading method and in fact the concepts of what teaching means make the results vulnerable to many criticisms. But because these conclusions were based on a comparative study in the classroom, they did provide evidence which is helpful in the allocation of an activity within a curriculum. This comparative study supported a trade of game time for case time, if planning as defined by concepts 2 and 3 is one of the teaching objectives of the course.

The Second Evaluation Experiment

For the two-class run for 1962, a more extensive experiment was designed to evaluate a broader spectrum of appropriate teaching objectives of the game. The measuring device was a series of multiple choice examinations concerning four small business situations. The Faculty discussed and defined nine concepts which gaming might communicate better than cases. As noted in Chapter II, five were statements associated with a concept of rational planning, and four were statements concerning present organizational behavior research findings. Two multiple choice tests concerning short cases were designed to evaluate the five concepts associated with planning. They involved testing the skill of the students in developing an appropriate set of goals and then selecting a consistent set of decision steps given their set of goals.

The multiple choice tests were developed to aid in grading and to introduce a more objective measure than the judgment of one individual. To support the quantitative data, the Faculty members involved in teaching the game classes were asked to compare their game students with their nongame students on their understanding of the nine concepts. An analysis of the examinations proved no discrimination between any possible grouping game or otherwise. The conclusion was reached that planning performance is too complex an activity to evaluate without independent judgment of a complete plan of analysis. A graduate student is able to create consistent plans in a multiple choice test almost without reference to the basic data.

The test concerned with the human relations concept provided some interesting results although they were not too conclusive. In one test the students were asked to rate the validity of fourteen principles of management using the following five classes: true, probably true, uncertain, probably false, and false, and their usefulness, with these five definitions: always useful, occasionally useful, uncertain, rarely useful, never. The game class had less extreme judgments than the nongame class on the basis of a chi square statistical test ($\alpha = 10\%$). This test might indicate a somewhat less naive approach to principles and might support the hypothesis that the simulation experience proved that less reliance should be placed on stereotyped solutions to organizational and human relations problems. The second test involved a case that described a small business group situation. (For grading purposes the real life outcome was known to the graders.) The students were requested to state whether ten statements about the group were true, uncertain, or false. Students involved in the game class seemed to predict more accurately the true life result. These tests suggest that the simulation experience induced a more sophisticated approach to problems and therefore support the aforementioned hypothesis. The evidence in either case is not too conclusive. As noted above, the main reason for continuing use of the game was the supporting opinion of the Faculty that gaming was desirable. The experimental design and the process of defining possible teaching objectives did provide a well-defined basis for evaluating the potential of games subjectively, and these factors convinced the Faculty more than experimental data might have.

A "Need for Achievement" Trial

The 1963 experiment was stimulated by a seminar on decision making which discussed Professor McClelland's concept of "need for achievement" as a predictor of good managers.[3] The seminar decided that individuals having a high need for achievement would probably be better risk-aversion decision makers and would tend to plan more thoroughly than those with a low need for achievement. Assuming that most of the individuals in the MBA curriculum had about the same aspiration level for success, this achievement conjecture seemed to be one that could be tested in the game environment. The rationale of the hypothesis to be tested was, in brief: an individual with a high need for achievement would also have a great aversion to failure and would thus take less risk. His high need for achievement combined with a high aspiration level would encourage him to do a great deal of analysis and he would take slow incremental steps in the appropriate direction. The low need for achievement and high aspiration level individual would be quite willing to gamble in hopes of making a quick success; the risk of failure is not too important in his value system. Conjecture was that this individual using intuition or hunch might change radically and perhaps not do as well as the individual having a high need for achievement.

To test this hypothesis, firms were formed according to their need for achievement level as measured by Professor McClelland's test. The inference was that the firms with the high need for achievement would not change price or hunt as much in their

[3] D. C. McClelland, *The Achieving Society*; D. C. McClelland, "Achievement Motivation Can Be Developed."

budget-making procedures as those firms with the low need for achievement; thus, the decision makers of a firm were measured for consistency. To evaluate the hypothesis, thirty men of a ninety-man class were evaluated on a "need for achievement" test and grouped into three high-need firms and three low-need firms. The firms were not aware of their composition; two experimental firms were placed in each of three six-firm industries for the play of the game. During the game, the number and size of changes in budget levels and prices for each of the 18 firms in the industries were recorded. Of the six control firms only three seemed to have altered their plans differently than the nonexperimental firms. Two high-need-for-achievement firms produced only about 55% of the changes one of the low-need-for-achievement firms made. However, the experimental firms as a group did not differ statistically significantly from the 12 control firms. An adequate sample was not available to discriminate adequately in such a narrow range of individual aspirations. It would seem that the students were relatively homogeneous in their desires. The topic could well be the subject for further research.

A Statistical Search As a Basis for Further Research

The 1964 game investigation was a statistical analysis of student game performance and of other measures relating to the student's intellectual ability and social position. The Educational Testing Service Admission Test for Graduate Study in Business scores, student undergraduate grades, and HBS grades for each student were compared with game performance to determine if there existed any discernible relationships between performance in the game and the normal standards of success, namely, profit or sales. In order to provide a broad basis for feasible relationships, students for all firms were selected at random. This study was designed to be used for a more extensive experiment to consider what criteria for grouping would be most appropriate given the student data obtained during the academic term preceding the formation of the firms. In addition to test scores and grades, background information was coded, for instance, marital status, service, age, and work experience.

Thirty-five factors which seemed important and performed an extensive correlation analysis were developed. There was evidence of some relation between three of the courses and the success in simulation. The firms that had two or more students who performed well in the Finance, Production, and Control courses, by and large did better in the simulation than the other firms. Another interesting factor was that the firms which had similar test scores and college grades often seemed to do better than the firms with a broad range of test scores and grades. To evaluate the impact of each student having high ability, each firm was compared with the individual student's performance. This analysis indicated that in no instance did one individual seem to influence success (two or more were required), but if there was only one with high ability, there was some correlation with firm failure. It appeared that a homogeneous combination of firm members' talent was "better" than diversity. This may indicate that the task is more than one man's job. The results of the undesigned statistical analysis provided a basis for the 1965 research design but, on the basis of the data, no strong conclusions could be reached concerning how to group firms or what student characteristics aid a firm's performance. It appeared that the homogeneity of the group and the firm's relationship with its Faculty members might have as much significance and influence in the outcome as the particular selection of students.

1965 Game Research at the Harvard Business School

The 1965 game experiments were aimed at improving the learning potential of the game. In the view of most players, learning comes predominantly from the organizational experiences of working with teammates in making decisions rather than from the specific nature of the decisions they are asked to make.[4] It comes from reflecting about their actions and experiences and from trying to justify their decisions and the resulting economic consequences to Faculty members who serve as boards of directors to the firms. Learning is also enriched by assignments relating to the game in other courses before, during, or after the students play. Where sim-

[4] Dill and Doppelt, "The Acquisition of Experience in a Complex Management Game," pp. 30–46.

ulation games are embedded into a curriculum, Faculty behavior is at least as important as characteristics of the simulation model in stimulating learning. There are still many unanswered questions about how to involve Faculty effectively and about how to organize the players as firms in a complex simulation exercise. Many choices exist, and many have been tried, but with relatively little investment to measure the effects of different approaches on what the player learns. This study attempted to provide data to assist the game designer in making the best use of Faculty and firm organization. The study in essence tested a few ideas on how to help players learn.

The first of these concerned the "attitude" which students adopted at the beginning of the game. If some players were asked to write about what they intended to learn from the experience before they began to play, would this affect performance, satisfaction, or post-game testimony about what had been learned? It was hoped that even a brief assignment asking some of the players to describe their personal learning agenda would lead them to be more experimental and more reflective as they played the game.

The second idea was intended to reinforce the first. It had been demonstrated in a variety of settings that one of the most productive ways to have Faculty members involved in a management simulation exercise was to have them serve as boards of directors to the player firms. Many methods for establishing boards have been used, including the teaming of Faculty members with top-level executives from the local business community.[5] Relatively little has been done, though, to control the posture that boards adopt in dealing with the teams. This study was designed to measure the effects of three different Faculty orientations as board members: one group of directors to stress profits, another to stress experimentation in group organization for decision making, and the third to stress activities that would maximize the learning which teams could take from the game into other courses. As the results of the study show, however, a different but equally significant question arose—one concerning the ability of Faculty members to assume and of students to recognize and accept different board orientations.

[5] K. J. Cohen et al., *The Carnegie Tech Management Game,* pp. 77–85.

The third concern was with the assignment of men to firms. Earlier studies suggest that firm performance is independent of firm averages on aptitude and certain personality tests and that satisfaction is higher among students when they have a voice in selecting and organizing the firms in which they play. But many other facets have not been explored.

One possibility, based on recent arguments that the best way to train managers to work as a team is to train them as a team, led to a comparision of experienced versus newly formed groups. During the term preceding play, all the students had participated in an experimental, group-based human relations course. In setting up firms for the game, it was possible to keep some of the groups intact as firms and to contrast them with firms that were formed without reference to prior group assignments. It was felt that experienced groups might get off to a faster start and might work together more effectively in the game.

With the firms that were not organized on the basis of prior group assignments, a second proposition was explored. Firms were assembled so that their members were homogeneous in ability or in past scholastic performance. It has been argued by some that equality of ability among members of a firm would stimulate learning by providing greater equality of opportunity to share in the jobs that the firm must do. Hence, homogeneous groups would show greater satisfaction, better performance, and more learning.

Experimental Design

The organization of the first-year MBA Program had some convenient experimental design features. At the beginning of the year, the 670 students were divided into 7 equally sized classes, each of which was to represent the geographic origins, academic backgrounds, and social makeup of the total group. Each of the ninety-man classes met together throughout the first year with a single set of Faculty. These arrangements gave a base against which to introduce variations in team organization and in the roles of Faculty members as directors for the student firms.

For students in three of the seven classes, the assignment to firms perpetuated groups that had been set up at random the term before in the organizational behavior course. These groups faced a change in mission, but not in membership. For students in the other four classes, the assignment to firms was made with the objective of contrasting homogeneous teams with different levels of capability. The specific measures varied from class to class; but essentially men were matched within teams on prior undergraduate performance, graduate entrance examination scores, and first-term grades at HBS.

Each of the seven classes was split into three independent industries of from six to seven firms, and each industry had its own Faculty board of directors to introduce the simulation exercise and to guide the students as they tried to master it. Each board was to encourage rational play and reflection on experience, but each of the three boards within a given class had a different emphasis to impart. One was to stress profits. A second was to encourage experimentation in team organization and decision making. The third was to emphasize the use of the game to exploit learning opportunities which had implications for future courses or the students' job goals.

Students' attitudes and understanding of the simulation by questionnaires before, during, and after play were sampled. An attitude questionnaire to poll reactions to team assignments and to measure students' anxieties was given at the beginning of the game. After the fourth move, four classes were given an ungraded examination to test their understanding of the simulated environment and of the rules for play. At the same time, the other three classes were asked to describe their learning agenda: improvements in knowledge, skill, perspective, and attitudes that they would like to accomplish in the game.

At the conclusion of play, all classes filled out the attitude questionnaire again and took a new test on their understanding of the simulation and the rules of play. They also completed a questionnaire, rating what they thought they had learned. Each Faculty board documented the progress and behavior of their firms in accordance with a standard set of instructions. These responses, along with the economic results attained by the student firms, comprise the data base for the study.

Learning Agenda and Their Effects

The effort to get students to think out their agenda for learning from the game was disappointing. Although information about the game was available from second-year students and although the game was looked on positively by most students as they began to play, students' lists of potential learning were not particularly rich or specific. These agenda did not read as if the students set forth much prior thought or personal commitment. No relationship was found between either the length or content of the pre-game learning agenda and players' satisfactions, performance, and post-game testimony about learning.

Experience on a smaller scale with business executives, subsequent to this experiment, suggests that pre-game discussion and analysis of what players hope to learn can be valuable, but that the effort must go beyond simply writing agenda. Ways must be found to review the agenda against the opportunities that the game will provide and to refer back to the agenda as play progresses.

The Influence of Faculty Boards

The reason for asking the Faculty directors to emphasize different aspects of gaming was to measure the effects of these differences on how students approached and reacted to the game. The boards that stressed profits were to make it clear they would grade the teams on their success as money makers. Students were to be measured, not by style and strategies, but by economic results. The boards that stressed experimentation in team organization and operation took a more direct counseling role. They were to grade students by how well they functioned as teams, with little or no emphasis on actual economic results. The boards that stressed using the game as a vehicle for long-term learning were supposed to encourage radical variations in students' play, using the game less as a competitive economic exercise and more as a setting in which each man could practice analytical approaches that would improve his future capabilities as a manager.

The differences in role were subtle and, after the game, students were checked by questionnaire about the role they *perceived* their board to play. Later it was found that the communication of intended roles had not gone according to plan. Table III provides a concise statement of differences between intention and result.

The profit message was most consistently received. The experimental, counseling role seems to have been communicated effectively by only one of the seven boards who were asked to take that emphasis. The emphasis on future learning was communicated with reasonable consistency. It was not clear from our data how

TABLE III

Communication of Intended Faculty Roles

Message Intended	*Message Received by Individual*				
	Profit	*Experiment*	*Future Learning*	*None*	*Total*
Profit	112	7	19	25	163
Experiment	48	27	45	33	153
Future Learning	62	27	74	15	178
Total	222	61	138	73	494

Interpretation: χ^2 of equal opportunity = 76.5
Overall R (message intended/message received) = 0.24
Overall R (message received/message intended) = 0.06

much of the failure to communicate rested on the Faculty's inability to assume a role and how much on the unreceptiveness of the students. Because the model itself tends to reinforce a competitive interest in profits, both factors were probably involved.

The HBS Faculty seems to accommodate best to a profit-oriented role, and the students seem to anticipate this is the role they should take. Counseling by Faculty on how to make decisions was misunderstood and resented by students as interference with their freedom as "managers" in the game. The students expected the Faculty to question their plans and actions critically after the fact, but they did not want to be limited in their freedom to frame plans and try different courses of action.

The moderate success of the future-oriented emphasis by Faculty boards suggests, though, that directors can do more than evaluate the short-term profitability of student actions. By relating profit-seeking activity within the game to broader business questions from outside the game, Faculty directors can help students generalize the game experience in ways that will be helpful after play is over. If this sort of reflective activity can be fostered during the game, it is felt that students will take more from the game. Finding ways to promote transfer of game experience into subsequent course and job experiences is important to show that investments in simulation exercises are justified.

Experienced versus Newly Formed Teams

Predicting that experienced teams would have an advantage over newly formed teams was not confirmed. In three of the ninety-man classes, teams perpetuated groups that had worked together during the previous term in an experimental human relations course. In the other four classes, teams covering other criteria were assembled in ways that broke up groupings from the human relations course.

Thus, while all players had received the same human relations training, only those from three of the classes could apply what they had learned to the same groups they had been trained with. It was expected that firms with a previous history of working together might start with a better attitude toward each other and, over the course of the exercise, maintain higher levels of satisfaction with the group and produce better results. On the other hand, since team assignments in both the human relations course and the game were involuntary, many individuals might feel frustrated in their inability to change group membership when starting the game. Such frustration might have negative effects on satisfaction, performance, and learning. The hypothesis reached was that the advantages of continued association would outweigh the disadvantages.

The results suggest that, instead, advantages and disadvantages may cancel each other. Experienced firms were neither higher nor more variable in pre-game satisfaction than newly established firms. Throughout the game, changes in level of satisfaction on a variety of measures were comparable in direction and magnitude for both kinds of firms. While firms with prior history together showed slightly less of a decline in satisfaction with the way they worked together as a team than did newly established firms, the difference was not large enough to be significant. Experienced groups also failed to show any superiority in profit and sales performance or in the amounts they reported having learned from participation in the game.

Generalizations from the results—or lack of results—are difficult. Perhaps differences were washed out by the sharp change in task assignments between the human relations course and the game. Both established and newly formed groups faced new levels of challenge and uncertainty as they entered the simulation exercise. In the face of the task change, specific approaches learned during the human relations course may not have seemed to apply. The results cast doubt on arguments for training managers as teams unless this team training would make direct and specific reference to the environment and challenges that the team would face when it returned to its regular job.

Organizing Firms by Ability

One alternative method of grouping was based on intellectual ability as measured by undergraduate grades, scores on the E.T.S. Admission Test for Graduate Study in Business, and first-term grades at the Harvard Business School. A different combination was used in each of four classes to separate the class into firms of above-average, average, and below-average ability:

1. First-term Harvard Business School grades alone.
2. Predicted first-year Harvard Business School grades. (Predictions were made from an estimated equation that was derived on the basis of regression analysis for recent classes. The equation relates Admission Test for Graduate Schools of Business scores and undergraduate grades to first-year Harvard Business School grades and has predicted accurately about 72% of all recent student grades.[6])
3. A comparison of first-term grades with predicted grades. (All students whose grades were appreciably higher than the predictor were considered overachievers—above average. Those whose grades were appreciably lower were considered underachievers, or below average, and the remainder achievers or average.)

[6] R. S. Rosenbloom, "A Progress Report on a Study of First-Year Grades for the Experimental Section."

4. A combination of first-term grades and achievement level. (This included firms that represented both high-grade performance and overachievement, average-grade performance and overachievement, low-grade performance and overachievement, high-grade performance and average achievement, etc. This method of classification was intended to test the discriminating power of two measures versus one.)

Several measures were used to compare team performance: operating profit, sales volume, and Faculty appraisals. Because teams played against three slightly different computer models of the environment, all sales and profit results were normalized for each of the models. Table IV shows profit and sales positions for the above-average, and below-average groups (with the established groups, holding over from the human relations course, as controls). Profits were significantly better for the above-average groups and significantly poorer for the below-average groups. Average groups did about as well as the randomly assigned former human relations teams. The picture for sales is less clear than for profits, perhaps because of controllable factors in the simulation. It was much easier for teams in general to generate sales than profits.

TABLE IV

Normalized Profit and Sales Performance Against Ability Measures

		Ability Classification of Teams			
		Above Average	*Average*	*Below Average*	*Randomized Ability (Control)*
Normalized Profits	Upper Third	13 [a]	11	3	19
	Middle Third	6	13	9	18
	Lower Third	0	15	9	22
Normalized Sales	Upper Third	11	9	3	23
	Middle Third	5	14	9	18
	Lower Third	3	16	9	18

[a] Entries indicate number of teams.

Table V shows results from the pre-game and post-game attitude questionnaires. These results suggest that grouping individuals on the basis of ability or talent affects what they learn from the game. Players at the start were fairly equally satisfied with the game as part of their curriculum, but over the course of the game satisfaction held up much better for the above-average groups than for the average, below-average, or control groups. This may reflect superior performance, but it may also mean that only the above-average groups had the spark of leadership and individual initiative which generate and sustain morale.

The talent difference had no connection with understanding the basic rules of play or with the size and complexity of learning agenda. Learning objectives for the groups were similar, and all seemed to understand the rules equally well. The above-average groups, though, used their knowledge to better effect.

What do the results mean? In the initial stages, any simulation game poses first of all an intellectual task to learn the rules and discriminate among masses of information, and second an organizational task to adjust to others on the team and develop a decision-making style. The above-average students were able to adapt faster than their classmates; and this capacity made them more confident, more satisfied, and less anxious from the start of the game. The below-average groups seemed to be overwhelmed by the task. Within the group few had leadership capability to show the way through early problem situations. Early dissatisfaction with poor results led in turn to reduced effort, either in trying to learn the simulation or to cope with the problems that the competitive situation posed. The end result was both poor performance and low satisfaction.

The differences in abiilty, while not affecting pre-game aspirations to learn, did affect post-game statements about what was learned. All groups claimed they learned about the same concerning the interrelationship of functional activities in the business firm. On methods of analyzing data and on evidence of learning from their experience, the above-average groups claimed they had more to show than the below-average or control groups. The measurements of post-game learning were crude, but evaluation does sug-

TABLE V

Average Measures of Individual Attitudes and Perceptions Against Ability Level of Group

Ability Level of Group	*Attitudes*						*Pre-Game Learning Agenda (Median Length)*	*Post-Game Claims of Learning*		
	Satisfaction with Game		*Satisfaction with Results*		*Satisfaction with Group*			*About Functions of Firm*	*About Analysis of Data*	*About Learning from Experience*
	Before	*After*	*Before*	*After*	*Before*	*After*				
Above Average	7.4	6.9 [a]	6.4 [a]	5.9 [a]	8.0 [a]	7.2 [a]	63	6.1	5.6 [a]	5.8 [a]
Average	7.0	6.2	5.7	5.3	7.2 [a]	6.3	56	6.4	5.0	5.7 [a]
Below Average	7.0	6.1	5.3	5.7	7.1 [a]	6.3	58	6.3	5.3	4.9
Randomized (Control)	7.0	6.0	5.8	5.3	7.6	6.5	62	6.4	5.0	5.1
	.18 [b]	.01	.004	.06	.001	.001		.41	.17	.09

[a] "t" test value significant at .10 level or better for difference between group measures and control group measures.
[b] Probability all grouping the same by F-test noted below each column.

gest that high satisfaction and a high sense of learning from the simulation experience do go together.

Some of the differences between the high-ability and low-ability groups may have stemmed from the transparency of the assignments. Because high performers and overachievers tended to be people recognized within the class as discussion leaders in other courses, the class knew that team assignments were not made at random. There was some resentment toward the game administrators for what was perceived by the students as an obvious bias in the groupings.

The anticipated differences between various classes, based on the measure of ability that was used to set up teams, proved too subtle to pull from the data. It can be noted only that the class which was sorted both on measures of overachievement and underachievement, and on academic record, produced as was expected the most and the least profitable firms in the game.

Conclusion

The early history of simulation exercises seems to parallel the early history of many other educational innovations: textbooks, the case method, and programmed instruction. In each case there was a mixture of fear and hope that the technique could serve by itself, providing students with the resources to learn with a minimum of active planning or guidance from the instructor. Simulation exercises seemed particularly appealing because they permitted bringing the real world into the classroom in ways that had not been possible before and because they proved exciting and engrossing to the students who would participate.

What has been learned in general—and what this study was particularly designed to confirm—is that simulation experiences in themselves are not enough. In fact, some of the very things that make such experiences engrossing and exciting may diminish their educational effectiveness. The competitive aspects of a management game, for example, do arouse motivation and do help sustain effort. But they may also detract from long-term learning by leading students to play conservative strategies instead of experimenting with new approaches, by teaching students to emphasize short-term profits within the game context instead of building and trying to achieve long-term strategic plans, and by influencing students to let anxieties about relative performance and grades interfere with efforts to learn.

This study has tried to highlight two of the important factors in making simulation experiences more productive from the standpoint of learning. First, the way in which teams are organized has been stressed. Keeping groups together simply because they have worked together before does not seem to enhance what they get from the game. Grouping them so that they are homogeneous in ability or prior performance has proved to have serious drawbacks. Second, it has been found especially detrimental to both satisfaction and performance to make teams that reflect obvious differences in potential compete against each other in the same industry.

The results of this study have led to a recommendation against any method of grouping that puts the weaker members of the class together on teams and to a suggestion that each team should have at least a couple of men with above-average ability or leadership potential. To the greatest extent possible, in order to remove student resentment against having team structure imposed on them, the students themselves should decide how team assignments should be made and how teams should be organized.

One other concern was experimentation with the role of faculty boards of directors. The results of the experiment emphasizes that the role which is chosen should be not only one that the faculty members can play with comfort and conviction and one that the students will see as legitimate, but also one that is relevant to the game and to the general environment of the educational institution. In an MBA program similar to the one used in this study, the conclusion is that the faculty member serves better as a critic and interrogator of the role that the students are trying to assume than as an active counselor or consultant on how to manage. The role can be augmented usefully by encouraging students to look at their activities in the game against the perspective of their future aspirations as business executives.

The restrained role of interrogator and critic is most appropriate when the amount of time a faculty director can spend with his team is limited. If the director can work closely enough with the team to understand the simulated environment, team organization, and the strategic plans as well as the team members do, he may be able to win their respect and trust as a counselor. Otherwise his advice too often seems like irrelevant interference.

With the improvement of simulation techniques and languages and with expansions both in the capacity of computers and in the flexibility of arrangements by which students can interact with the machine, educational institutions can look ahead to simulation games that will be many stages more complex and realistic than the ones in existence today. At the same time, the future of simulation in education probably rests less on technical developments than it does on efforts to tie the use of models more closely into the total curriculum and the total environment of student-faculty relationships.

Future Game Research

A strong stimulus to recent game research has been the need among business researchers for a laboratory environment.[7] The classical economic model of a completely rational decision maker has not proved to be an effective operational model, and a dramatic growth in research efforts on decision-making behavior of economic managers is presently manifest as evidenced by the variety of recently published works on how organizations make decisions.[8] This research has shifted from abstract model building to documentation of the inputs the decision maker requires, how he formulates the alternatives, the values he places on the alternatives, and the estimates of success he makes prior to his selection of his plan of action. This shift has increased the need to observe decision makers. The theme of current and future research, then, is a blending of the concepts of economic, psychological, and statistical decision theory into those of more operational theory.

This research activity is linked to gaming by the very desirable

[7] An interesting unpublished paper by Martin Shubik on "Gaming, Costs and Facilities," outlines a proposal for developing such a laboratory. This study is based on survey data on uses of games.

[8] Cyert and March, *A Behavioral Theory of the Firm*; Collins and Guetzkow, *A Social Psychology of Group Process for Decision Making.*

experimental attributes a simulation game has for observing decision making.[9] First it is a controlled environment, since all decision variables are defined and identified before the fact. Second, one can control the communications between participants by observing and further eliminating unknown variables in the environment. The makeup of the groups and the information state of each group can be defined in a way that they do not seem to be part of an experiment but rather a simulated real-life problem. One can coach a team to perform desired activities for observing the response of other teams. It is relatively easy to measure the information upon which an individual bases his decisions, and one can obtain expected outcomes of the decision-making process from the individual.[10] In a sense, the decision maker can be placed in a completely controlled economic environment without being aware of the control. The motivation of peer groups and the stimulus of the game as a challange make the student a very serious rational decision maker in this controlled environment. Data can thus be acquired on a continuing decision-making process.

On the basis of experimentation, this study concludes that with careful design a wide spectrum of studies on the nature of decision making and information processing can be conducted concurrently with a management simulation game primarily designed for developing managers. This investigation supports others that the simulation model is not all-important, but the firm organization and faculty role are quite significant aspects of the learning environment. Thus, given similar organizations and faculty attention, the simulated environment could be modified to measure desired factors. Economic parameters in the models have been varied simultaneously eliciting no student response because of the variation. It seems likely that the model and quantity of information

[9] Examples of recent research with games are:
B. M. Base, "Business Gaming for Organizational Research."
G. H. Symonds, "A Study of Management Behavior by Use of Competitive Business Games."
T. R. Hoffman, "Programmed Heuristics and the Concept of Par in Business Games."
M. Shubik, "A Business Game for Teaching & Research Purposes."

[10] For an extended discussion see E. M. Baff et al., "The Potential of Business Gaming Methods in Research," p. 472.

could be structured as Shubik suggests: to gain insight and to establish theories of decision making as an ongoing aspect of most complex gaming activities. A positive goal of present game designers should be to develop simulation games for teaching and research.

Appendix A

HBS Management Simulation Instructions to Participants

The Management Simulation is a laboratory experience in decision making under uncertainty. It will involve you in the problem of developing and implementing an economic strategy in an ongoing business. You and three of your classmates will manage one of five manufacturing firms which compete in a consumer goods industry. The demand for your firm's products, which will compete with products of four similar firms in your industry, will be dependent on your products' price, quality, and amount and timing of your marketing expenditures. After you have become familiar with the market and the available resources for your firm, your first task will be to formulate a competitive strategy for your firm.

The bulk of the simulation will be given to the implementation of this strategy in the simulated environment. This implementation will include setting prices for your products, determining their quality, scheduling their production, making allocations for their promotion, and financing your firm's operations. The end product of your analysis will be a plan for a quarter of the year's operation of your firm, in the form of a decision set.

After each set of decisions you will receive the results of your firm's operations for the quarter in the form of reports. Exhibit I is an example of the decision form. Sample reports are shown in Exhibits II–V. This information will permit you to evaluate your performance and to improve your understanding of your firm's competitive environment.

Copyright © 1965 by the President and Fellows of Harvard College. Revised 1966; 1967.

One of your primary tasks in managing your firm will be to acquire information on which to base your decisions. Basically, you have four sources from which to draw.

Prior to making your first decisions, you will receive reports covering four periods of past history of your firm. These reports will provide background information on your firm's operations from which you can discern how the production phase functions and observe the influences of seasonality on demand.

Second, these instructions explain the general range of the determinants of demand, as well as explaining how you may schedule production for your products and finance your firm's operations.

Third, your most important source of information will be the quarterly reports you will receive after each period of decision making. These reports, which will be in the same form as the initial history of your firm, will give full and precise information on your firm's operations. Your firm and the others within your industry will also receive identical reports on industry operations as a whole. Data, such as your competitors' total sales revenue, prices and financial data, which would be public knowledge in real life, will be reported accurately; however, data, such as product sales volume, product quality, and marketing expenditures, which would not be public knowledge, will be given only approximately.

Fourth, you will have the opportunity to purchase market research information for any product you are currently selling or would like to sell.

Thus at the beginning of the simulation, you will have relatively little information about your market or your competition. Although the simulation's design incorporates many general characteristics of actual industries, it is not a reproduction of any specific industry. Since many distinctive aspects of your individual market will be created by your actions and those of your competitors, you must analyze the gross data to understand your industry's characteristics in order to create and implement a successful strategy.

After becoming familiar with the introductory materials, your group is expected to decide on objectives for your firm and to formulate operating policies designed to achieve your objectives. You will be able to develop more detailed and perhaps more useful operating policies or strategies as you gain more knowledge about your industry. However, one of the most effective approaches has proven to be an attempt to formulate plans early in the simulation to identify what you do not know and to quickly familiarize yourself with the data. The simulation is so designed that any number of different strategies can be successful (e.g., high volume—low price, low volume—high price). The particular objectives you adopt should be appropriate for your firm's specific competitive environment. A careful digestion of these instructions and the four quarters of historical data on the operation of your firm should provide an adequate basis to develop appropriate tentative objectives. How nearly you achieve your objectives is dependent on how well you analyze the available information and prepare a plan of action which is consistent with your strategy. As you will note in the following instructions, fluctuating behavior will be penalized. Your success will be dependent, in large measure, not so much on what particular objectives you adopt, but rather on how well you plan ahead so that your individual moves achieve a cumulative momentum toward your objectives.

Determinants of Demand

Total demand for an industry's products is determined externally by general economic conditions and internally by industry activity. The external influence comes from seasonal variations and general economic conditions. The Income Statement (see Exhibit II) contains a seasonally adjusted business index. Thus, the business index, reflecting consumer disposable income, represents the general economic level and not the seasonal influences present in this consumer goods industry. The business index is calculated as if there is no seasonal influence in the market. An improvement in the business index of 5% may be offset by the normal seasonal downswing. The indices are precise for present and past periods but the accuracy of the forecasted indices decreases as they become longer range. The normal level of economic activity is about 700. In the absence of counteracting influences, such as price cuts or increased marketing expenditures, market demand swings upward and downward with the index. When the business index is falling, consumers are more price conscious than they are when the index is rising.

The internal influence of industry activity, however, is a more important determinant of demand than external economic developments. How effectively the industry as a whole exploits its potential market is dependent on the total marketing expenditures of the firms and the extent to which consumer needs are satisfied. Since potential customers differ in attitudes toward price, the industry can best exploit its market by offering products with a diverse set of prices. Thus it is im-

TABLE OF CONTENTS

Appendix A

Determinants of Demand 139
Marketing Insights 141
  Number of Products 141
  Price 141
  Product Quality 141
  Product Development 142
  Promotion 142
  Marketing 143
  Market Research 143
  Available Goods 144
Production 144
  Plant Equipment 145
    Increasing Plant and Equipment 145
    Semi-Fixed Costs Included in Factory Overhead 146
  Inventories 146
  Labor Force 146
    Experienced Men 147
    Transferred Men 147
    Hiring and Firing Men 148
    Idle Men 148
  Scheduling Production 148
  Warehousing and Shipping 150
Introducing a New Product 150
  To Add a New Product 150
  To Replace a Current Product with a New Product 151
Finance 151
  90-Day Unsecured Loans 152
  90-Day Secured Loans 152
  90-Day Distress Loans 153
  One-Year Loans 153
  Five-Year Notes 153
  Common Stock 154
  Securities 154
Summary of Time Impacts 155
The Reports 156
  Exhibit I—Decision Form 158
  Exhibit II—Income Statement 160
  Exhibit III—Balance Sheet 164
  Exhibit IV—Product Statement 168
  Exhibit V—Industry Report 172
Appendix 1—including Exhibits VI through X 171

portant to consider the total market structure and activity when formulating your business strategy.

The demand for any given product of a firm is dependent upon its price, its quality relative to that of similarly priced products, its promotion and marketing and product development expenditures, and its availability for sale. The best method of identifying your competitors is to rank all products in an industry by price; those closest to your own are your keenest competitors. There is relatively little competitive interaction between products differing widely in price. The product number has no significance.

Growth in demand for your products is dependent on your expenditures in promotion, marketing and product development. Promotion expenditures are for market penetration of a new product or an improved existing product. Promotion expenditures are only used when you intend to change your existing product mix and can be considered to cover costs of missionary salesmen, counter displays and dealer discounts to fill the pipeline of distribution. Marketing expenditures cover advertising accounts and normal promotion and selling expenses and are for the purpose of influencing the ultimate purchaser. Product development expenditures must be made continuously to maintain the market image of an established product as well as to make improvements in quality control, product design, styling and packaging.

Marketing Insights

The following information is a substitute for "hand-me-down" experience concerning the market an executive usually can obtain from his predecessors when he tackles a new job. You may assume that the following information is accurate, but you should not assume that it is complete.

Number of Products. Each firm may manufacture up to three products simultaneously. A change of more than 30% in the price of a product from one period to the next is considered by the market to be a change of product.

Price. A one per cent downward price change may result in an increase of two to five per cent in demand for a product. The full effects of a price increase are felt at once, while those of a decrease develop more slowly. Demand for a product priced beyond $44 will not support the expense of keeping a product alive. Products priced below $4 will not bring a profitable return.

Product Quality. The quality of a product is determined by the amount of labor and material value put into the product in the manufacturing operations. Labor value is comprised of labor cost per unit in both the fabrication and assembly departments. Material value is subdivided into the cost per unit of purchased parts and the cost per unit of raw material. At a MINIMUM, products must have $.60 worth of labor, of which $.40 must be fabricated and $.20 must be assembly; and $.90 worth of materials of which $.60 must be raw material and $.30 must be purchased parts. The following are examples of normal products for this market:

Fabrication Labor	$ .40	.75	1.05	1.40	2.40	3.60	4.50
Assembly Labor	.20	.40	.75	1.40	4.50	10.80	17.10
Raw Material	.60	.85	1.10	1.35	2.20	3.40	4.50
Purchased Parts	.30	.35	.40	.45	.60	.80	1.00
Quality Total	$1.50	2.35	3.30	4.60	9.70	18.60	27.10

The market is sensitive to the proportion of labor to material; the market accords full value to the costs of inputs within a normal range. Unusual proportions of labor to material are discounted in quality competition to create a market image based upon normal proportions.

A one per cent change in the cost per unit for a product may result in a one-half to three per cent change in demand, the larger change applying especially to large markup items, and the smaller to low price, low markup items. The consumer reacts quickly to changes. The effect of downward cost changes is even more rapid than that of upward ones.

Product Development. A normal low range of expenditures for product development is about $.30/unit per period for a $7.00 product and about $1.00/unit per period for a $25 product. A ten per cent increase may add as little as one-half per cent to the demand for a high-priced product. For already large budgets the effects of further increases in product development expenditures become even less beneficial. Product development expenditures for one product enhance the market image of other products of a firm and thus establish a brand preference. One can consider product development as research and engineering costs which maintain the style and timeliness of your product. It normally takes two periods for customers to react to changed expenditures for product development.*

Promotion. Promotion expenditures are used for rapid penetration of the market with a new product or for an increase in sales of an ex-

* It is important to maintain these expenditures because eliminating them completely is interpreted by the market as product elimination in the near future and therefore sales are depressed.

isting product which is to be changed. Any price change over 5%, quality change over 15% or budget change in product development expenditures over 20% are examples of significant changes for which expenditures would be appropriate. A promotion expenditure should precede anticipated product innovations since it influences the distribution system and the effects of a promotion expenditure are not felt in the market until the period after the expenditure is made. If you plan to make significant changes in a product (such as a $.75 price increase for a $6.85 product), a well-timed promotion budget might increase the sales potential of your changed product by 24 to 30 per cent over a similar level of marketing expenditures. After a product is established, normal marketing expenditures accomplish routine promotion efforts and promotion expenditures should be discontinued. A firm's promotion efforts for one of its products to some extent enhances demand for its other products.

Marketing. The effects of changes in marketing expenditures are felt fairly quickly, with downward changes taking hold more quickly than upward ones. An increase in a relatively low marketing budget by ten per cent may result in an increase of as much as six or eight per cent in demand for a product. But a doubling of an already large budget (e.g., $700,000 per period) will result in as little as a three per cent increase. A firm's marketing efforts for one of its products to some extent enhances demand for its other products.

Market Research. A firm that plans to introduce a new product or modify an established product may purchase research of a test market nature to obtain information on potential demand. You may test the potential product unit sales for the four demand determinants or any combination thereof. The demand determinants are: price, quality (labor and materials value), marketing and product development expenditures. If you wish to modify an existing product, you may test one or more of these determinants. However, if you plan to use market research prior to introducing a new product or the first period a new product is on the market, you must test at least two determinants, one of which must be price.

To obtain such information, you must indicate on the decision sheet the prices, total cost per unit, product development, or marketing budget you are considering assigning to your new or changed product. When obtaining market information for a proposed product and you are willing only to buy information for one, two, or three determinants, the values for the unspecified determinants will be average figures for roughly similar products in your industry. For example, on a new product you might want to know the expected demand for a $18.00 product at $9.00 cost per unit with a marketing budget of $120,000 per quarter and be willing to spend $70,000 for this information. You would allocate the $70,000 to the new product market research budget and define the $18.00, $9.00 and $120,000 in the appropriate blanks. The product development budget for this product will be an average of the product development budgets of the four or five closest priced products. Similarly, when obtaining information for an existing product using fewer than four determinants, the values of the unspecified determinants will be those actually used in the period in which you obtain the market research data.

The range of costs for market research is as follows:

Number of Demand Determinants	*Market Research Budget*
one	$10,000– 50,000
two	40,000– 70,000
three	60,000– 90,000
four	80,000–120,000

Within each range, the relative size of the expenditure will usually determine the degree of accuracy of the market research information. Information will be less accurate at the lower end of the range than at the upper end. No market research information can be considered more than 90 per cent accurate and occasionally it will be completely noise. A higher expenditure within a given range assures a greater protection against pure random information.

Available Goods. Production volume from the assembly department during the current period, plus finished goods inventory on hand, determine goods available. Because sales are not at an even rate, you should produce an adequate amount to exceed the total orders received by about ten per cent. If a customer's order is not filled "at once" he usually will reorder a similar product offered by another firm and not come back.

Goods carried over from one period to another tend to become less salable, especially in the case of relatively high quality products. For instance, a one-period unit produced at $10.00 roughly matches in salability a newly manufactured unit costing only $9.40 (i.e., $.60 less). The obsolescence effect is not reflected in the accounting evaluation of inventory.

Production

The successful formulation of your firm's strategy will depend in part on your understanding of feasible alternatives for your manufacturing capacity. The attainment of your strategy will depend on how carefully you control the resources available. The following sections describe in detail what decisions are required for you to transform raw materials into finished goods available for sale in your market.

You will have to make decisions which include all the economic aspects of a production process. These will include deciding whether to maintain plant capacity or to expand it by purchasing plant and equipment, when to hire men or fire them, and how to assign men to the two departments of each product. Raw material and finished goods inventories are a function of this period and next period's production rate, which you will have to determine. There are costs both in terms of dollars and inefficiencies associated with changes in production rate, expanding plant capacity and changing the number of men available.

Plant Equipment

Plant and equipment depreciates at a rate of 2.5% per quarter. Depreciation is allocated to the individual products on the basis of direct labor hours and is listed as "Depreciation" in the Income Statements. To maintain a given plant value (and thus capacity), you must invest a sum each period equal to the depreciation loss. Plant and equipment *cannot* be sold. However, you can reduce your plant by allowing it to depreciate.

Increasing Plant and Equipment. You may increase your plant's labor capacity by investing $2,500 (above the amount needed to hold ground against depreciation) of plant and equipment for each desired additional worker. There is a time lag associated with a decision to increase the size of your plant. The costs of added plant and equipment will not be deducted from your firm's cash account until the first period after you have recorded your purchase on the decision sheet. The new capacity will not be available for production until the beginning of the second period after the entry period. Depreciation at the expanded rate will commence in the quarter you pay for the addition.

To illustrate, a firm with a $1,500,000 plant and a labor force of 600 wishes to increase their labor force to 650 men.

	Investment Required
To hold ground against depreciation (.025 × $1,500,000) =	$ 37,500
For new purchase (50 × $2,500) =	125,000
Total required purchase of plant and equipment	$162,500

If this decision is entered on the decision form for period six, the expenditures will be made in period seven, and the new capacity will be available for production during period eight.

Certain assessments are associated with the purchase of plant and equipment. The following table indicates their approximate magnitude.

Investment in plant and equipment	$125,000	200,000	1,000,000
Assessment	7,000	20,000	250,000

The increasing rate reflects the fact that a sudden expansion of facilities creates expenses such as maintenance, increased need for expediting material and the interruption with normal activities.

The above costs are allocated to individual products proportionately to direct labor hours and are included under "Maintenance" on the Income Statements (see Exhibit III). The assessment is paid in the decision period.

Semi-fixed Costs Included in Factory Overhead. For every product that you produce you will incur certain semi-fixed costs for supervision and maintenance (see Exhibit II). The cost of indirect labor is a function of the total labor hours utilized for each product. The cost of supervision depends on the number of workers assigned to a product and is approximately $160 per man. The cost of maintenance depends on the total number of units produced in the assembly department of each product line.

Inventories

A first in, first out policy is followed on all inventories. The value of the fabricated parts inventory is based on the raw materials cost per unit plus the fabrication labor cost per unit. Similarly the value of the assembly department work-in-process inventory and of the finished goods inventory is based on fabricated parts costs, plus purchased parts cost per unit and assembly labor cost per unit. If all inventory from a previous period is not utilized in a given period, its next period value is a weighted average of the old inventory plus inventory purchased or produced during the period.

Labor Force

Your total work force should have an approximate ratio of one man for each $2,500 of plant. You may employ an excess of labor, but when the excess reaches approximately eight per cent of the above ratio, added men interfere with the normal production process. This interference results in productivity losses which soon cancel the potential output of the additional labor. All departments lose this productivity in proportion to the number of men assigned.

Employees must be assigned separately to each department of each product. The number of men needed within a department to produce at a given rate is dependent on the labor cost per unit, and the degree of efficiency of the men assigned.

Experienced Men. Men who have been assigned previously to a department of a product produce 500 hours of work per quarter at a rate of $1.80 per hour. For example, if you have scheduled 8,000 units of production with a department, and the labor cost per unit is $5.40, you would need 48 men (three hours per unit × 8,000 units ÷ 500 hours per man).

You may schedule in advance any number of overtime hours up to 25% of your total number of productive hours in a department for a product. In the above example, if only 44 men were previously assigned and no additional men were to be hired, 2,000 hours of overtime would have to be scheduled in order to meet the production rate. Overtime labor is paid $3.00 per hour for assembly and $3.60 per hour for fabrication. However, the extra cost of overtime labor is not reflected in the labor value of the product; each overtime labor hour adds only $1.80 labor value to the product. Scheduled overtime is utilized as required to meet scheduled production levels. It will not be utilized until required to achieve the desired output with the assigned number of men. The cost of scheduled overtime is charged whether or not the overtime is actually required to meet the scheduled production rate.

Transferred Men. Men may be shifted from one department and/or product to another. You may make such transfers simply by recording on the decision sheet the total number of men you want to work in each department of each product for the period.

Transferred men will not work at full efficiency (i.e., 500 hours of work per quarter) in the first quarter after transfer. Their efficiency depends on the department from which they were transferred. The most efficient transfer is when workers from one department go to the corresponding department in another product. In such a transfer the men would work at about 95% efficiency in the period following the transfer. The next most efficient transfer occurs when workers transfer from one department to the other within the same product line. In such a transfer, men would work at about 85% efficiency. The least efficient transfer is from one department and product to another department and product. In such a transfer, workers would produce at about 75% efficiency. There is no way to indicate on the decision sheet where or how men are to be transferred. The model assumes that workers will be moved in the most efficient manner, and will therefore first transfer men within the same department whenever possible, then within a product line, and so forth. These estimates are provided to enable careful planning of production schedules and do not require any decisions on your part.

Hiring and Firing Men. If you wish to increase your work force, you may hire men at an initial cost of $200 per man. For their first quarter of work, they will work at an average of 55% of standard output. You may also release men at a severance cost of $50 per man. As with transferred men, workers are hired or fired to or from a specific department of a specific product. Nonassigned men (idle men) cannot be fired. Hiring or firing requires an additional entry on the decision sheet, while transferring men requires only changing the number of men assigned to each department. Hired men should also be included in the total number of men assigned to each department.

Idle Men. If there are more men employed than the total number assigned to the products, the excess men are assigned to a "pool" of idle men that are paid the usual wage, $1.80/hour. Men from this "pool" are available to work in any department on any product at 85% efficiency the next quarter. Idle men are assigned to work in a department only after all possible transfers between departments and products are made. The charge for these idle men is apportioned in indirect labor costs of the products in direct proportion to direct labor hours utilized.

Scheduling Production

One of your managerial tasks will be to schedule production of your firm's products. Each decision period represents twelve weeks of productive capacity. The manufacturing process is divided into two stages, fabrication and assembly. The workers assigned to the fabrication department turn raw materials into fabricated parts; fabrication takes three weeks. The assembly department's work force combines these fabricated parts with purchased parts to produce the finished products; assembly takes two weeks. The diagram on page 149 shows this process together with the six classifications of inventory.

In scheduling the appropriate levels of production, you first must determine what production rates per product are needed to meet anticipated demand for this period and for the next period. Based on these production rates a sufficient number of raw materials and purchased parts to meet your production schedule for each product will

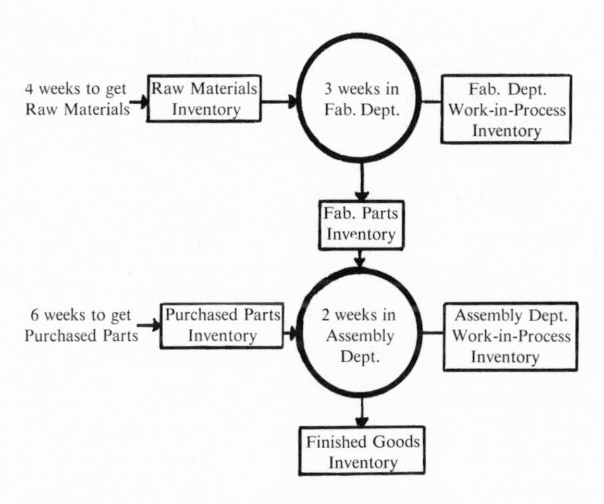

be purchased. Note as shown in the diagram there are known delays in acquiring raw materials and purchased parts. Therefore, accurate planning of the present and following period's desired production rates is essential to obtain sufficient inventories to prevent production stoppages due to inventory shortages. To maintain a constant level of production at the beginning of the period, you must have a four-week supply of raw materials and a six-week supply of purchased parts. An automatic purchaser will supply enough raw materials and purchased parts for this period and the beginning of next period. The amount of raw materials and purchased parts you order will be determined by the decisions you make concerning This Period's Production Rate and Next Period's Production Rate.

The amount of Raw Materials ordered for each product will be:

$$\begin{matrix}\text{This Period's Fab.} \\ \text{Production Rate}\end{matrix} - \begin{matrix}\text{Beginning} \\ \text{Inv. R.M}\end{matrix} + \begin{matrix}\tfrac{1}{3}\text{ Next Period's Fab.} \\ \text{Production Rate}\end{matrix}$$

The amount of Purchased Parts ordered for each product will be:

$$\begin{matrix}\text{This Period's Asm.} \\ \text{Production Rate}\end{matrix} - \begin{matrix}\text{Beginning} \\ \text{Inv. P.P.}\end{matrix} + \begin{matrix}\tfrac{1}{2}\text{ Next Period's Asm.} \\ \text{Production Rate}\end{matrix}$$

In scheduling the rates of production, you should be cognizant of the typical lag times in the total production process. The minimum lot size that can be withdrawn from the fabricated parts inventory is one week's assembly production. This, in effect, sets the minimum level on the size of your fabricated parts inventory. If you want to increase the rate of production in the assembly department, you must first build up the fabricated parts inventory by an appropriate amount. If you fail to do so, there will be a temporary work stoppage in the assembly department until the fabricated parts inventory builds up to one week of the higher level of production. Appendix A discusses in detail a procedure that may be used to forecast your production.

Warehousing and Shipping

Packing and shipping costs are about ten cents for each unit sold. Finished goods inventory carrying costs, including warehousing, insurance, etc., are approximately three cents per unit, plus one per cent of the inventory valuation per quarter. Raw material and purchased parts inventory carrying costs are about one and one-half per cent of the inventory valuation per period; fabricated parts and work-in-process inventory carrying costs are about three cents per unit. These costs are included under "Warehousing and Shipping" in the Income Statements.

Introducing a New Product

A new product may be introduced in one of two ways: (1) If the firm is manufacturing only two products, a third product may be added to the present product line. Each firm may manufacture up to three products simultaneously. (2) One of the current products may be phased out and replaced with a new product. A change of more than 30 per cent in the price of a product from one period to the next is considered by the market to be a change of product. The steps required to implement either of these alternatives are listed below.

To Add a New Product

(1) If market research is used prior to the introduction of the product or during the first period it is on the market you must test at least two of its four demand determinants (price, quality, marketing and product development expenditures), one of which must be price.
(2) If additional plant capacity must be purchased to support the product's production, it must be ordered at least two periods before it is available for production.
(3) Promotion expenditures should begin in the period prior to the one in which the product is introduced to the market. Unless substantial changes are made in the product's price, quality, or product development expenditures in the following period, it will be most effective to discontinue promotion expenditures and begin marketing expenditures.
(4) Product development expenditures should be started two periods before the product is introduced to the market.

To Replace a Current Product with a New Product

(1) Finished goods inventory of the old product must be drawn down to less than 100 items. Surplus raw materials and purchased parts may be sold by placing a minus one on the decision sheet under Production Rate Next Period or where Production Rates for both This Period and Next Period are zero. They will be sold at the previous average cost minus handling costs.
(2) The period following the one in which the old product's finished goods inventory is reduced to less than 100 items, production rates for the new product may be stated and its production started. The new product cannot be sold during this period and the price must be left blank on the decision form.
(3) Promotion expenditures should begin in the period prior to the one that the new product is introduced to the market.
(4) Product development expenditures should be continued during the entire transition period.

Finance

It will be necessary to finance your working capital and long-term capital needs. Your firm will require a minimum cash balance of at least 5% of the current quarter's cash disbursements. Several sources of funds are available. Internal sources of funds are provided by depreciation, profits after tax, and working capital changes. External funds can be provided by several forms of debt as well as by sale of common stock.

In setting your firm's objectives and in developing your competitive strategies to achieve these objectives, you must take into account the impact these goals and the policies will have on your need for funds and the ramification of your fund requirements on the stock price.

The effectiveness of the formulation and execution of your financial policies will be reflected in the market price of your firm's common stock. Eight factors are used in determining stock price:

(not necessarily listed in order of importance)

(1) the amount of earnings per share
(2) the recent pattern of earnings per share
(3) the firm's overall rate of return on total assets
(4) the dividend payout ratio
(5) the recent amount of dividend payments
(6) the ratio of debt to total capitalization
(7) the current index of economic activity
(8) the book value per share

The sources of external funds are:

(1) 90-day unsecured loans
(2) 90-day secured loans
(3) 90-day distress loans
(4) One-year loans
(5) Five-year notes
(6) Common stock

In general, the 90-day unsecured loans, one-year loans, and five-year notes will be granted only to those firms that meet fairly demanding tests of financial condition and earnings. All ratios used to test financial conditions are calculated on a pro forma basis; i.e., the ratios are calculated by using the numbers which are expected to appear on the balance sheet at the end of the coming quarter assuming that the loan in question is granted. If the financial position of a firm which has five-year notes outstanding subsequently deteriorates significantly, the notes outstanding may be retired prematurely in full.

The cash from requested loans is received at the beginning of the period. Cash from sale of stock and planned sale of securities is received at the end of the period. At either the beginning of the period or at the end, if additional cash is needed, securities will be automatically sold or 90-day secured or distress loans will be granted. Interest payments are made at the end of each quarter. Interest on loans incurred on the last day of the quarter will be paid in the next quarter.

(1) *90-day Unsecured Loans.* These loans take the form of 90-day notes with interest at an annual rate of 3% and will be available only when requested in advance. To be eligible for such loans a firm must meet the following requirements;
   (a) Liquidity—the firm's Quick Ratio, if loan is granted, must exceed 1.1. This is the ratio of cash plus securities plus accounts receivable plus size of requested loan to current liabilities (including loan payments due within one year) plus size of requested loan.
   (b) Profitability—profits must have been earned in the previous quarter.
   (c) Borrowing History—a firm cannot have 90-day unsecured loans in four consecutive periods.
(2) *90-Day Secured Loans.* These take the form of 90-day notes bearing interest at an annual rate of 10 per cent. Use of this source may be either planned or unplanned; i.e., emergency financing will be supplied automatically if planned financing is either inadequate or unavailable because the more rigorous financial tests associated with preferred sources of credit cannot be met. These funds will

be provided in amounts sufficient to keep the cash balance at a minimum of 5% of the quarter's cash expenditures. However, before unplanned loans are made, securities held by the company, if available, will be sold in amounts sufficient to meet cash requirements. To be eligible for a secured loan, a firm must meet the following requirement:

(a) Collateral—90-day secured loans must not exceed 80% of finished goods inventory plus accounts receivable. This ratio is calculated on a pro forma basis by estimating the values of the finished goods inventory plus accounts receivable at the end of the quarter.

(3) *90-Day Distress Loans.* When such loans are required, they will be made available in the form of 90-day notes bearing interest at an annual rate of 20 per cent. Such funds will be provided automatically and, therefore, need not be ordered. Securities will automatically be sold before distress loans are ordered.

Work-Out Program—Firms requiring distress loans must submit to the faculty board of directors a one-page report which outlines the firm's plans for returning to an acceptable financial position. Such a program might include planned sale of common stock in the near future.

(4) *One-Year Loans.* These are one-year notes bearing interest at an annual rate of 4½ per cent. These notes will be available only if ordered. To be eligible for one-year notes, a firm must meet the following tests:

(a) Liquidity—the firm's Quick Ratio if the loan is granted must exceed 1.2. This is the ratio of cash plus securities plus accounts receivable plus size of requested loan to current liabilities (including loan payments due within one year) plus size of requested loan.

(b) Profitability—profits must have been earned in at least three of the four previous quarters.

If the firm fails any of these tests no loan will be granted.

(5) *Five-Year Notes.* These are five-year notes at an annual interest rate of 6 per cent. These notes are available only if ordered. These notes require a quarterly sinking fund of 1/20th of the original issue, beginning in the sixth quarter following the issuance of the note with the unpaid balance retired in the 20th quarter. In the second period following the issuance of the note, an amount equal to the quarterly sinking fund is included in current liabilities. To be able to sell notes, a company must meet the following criteria:

(a) Fixed Charges Coverage—the average cash flow must exceed the fixed charges over the year ending with the current quarter. As computed by the following formula, the fixed charges coverage must be greater than one:

$$\frac{\text{Profit Before Taxes} + \text{Depreciation}}{\dfrac{\text{Sinking Fund}}{(1 - \text{Tax Rate})} + \text{Interest}}$$

Note: The profit before tax figure is an average of the current plus previous three quarter earnings before taxes; the depreciation figure is the current quarter's depreciation; the sinking fund figure is the current quarter's sinking fund plus the quarterly sinking fund if the note in question is issued; and the interest figure is the current quarter's interest plus the quarterly interest if the note is issued.

(b) Capitalization—five-year notes may not exceed 30 per cent of total assets.

If the firm is unable to meet these tests when its loan application is made, the firm will receive funds from other sources as required. If, during the life of a five-year note, a firm fails to meet 80% of either of the above tests (i.e., if the fixed charges coverage ratio is less than 80% or five-year notes exceed 44% of total assets), any five-year notes outstanding will be repaid immediately. If the firm does not have the cash to cover the accelerated unpaid principal, the firm will automatically have securities sold or be advanced the required amount in either a 90-day secured or distress loan.

(6) *Common Stock.* Companies may sell stock at any time specifically planned. To sell stock the firm must specify the net dollar amount it wants to raise. On the basis of the eight elements of value discussed earlier, a stock price as of the end of the period will be calculated. This price is then reduced to reflect the dilution of value by the increased number of shares outstanding. The number of new shares needed to obtain the desired funds is calculated to the nearest 100 shares. The cash from the stock sale will be available on the last day of the period. Securities cannot be purchased with funds from the sale of stock in the same period.

(7) *Securities.* Companies may invest in interest-bearing securities. These securities earn interest at an annual rate of 4 per cent. Purchase or sale of securities creates side costs of about one-half of one per cent of the transaction. Purchases or planned sales of securities are made at the end of the period; interest accumulates during the period securities are held or sold but not for the period in which they are purchased. Securities will automatically be sold if distress loans are required.

Summary of Time Impacts

	Prior Decision Period	*Present Decision Period* *Week* 1 2 3 4 5 6 7 8 9 10 11 12	*Future Decision Period*
Product			
Purchase Raw Material		X Y Deliver	
Purchase Purchased Parts		X Y Deliver	
Plant	X Decision to buy	Y Cash payment	Y Capacity available
Finance			
Planned Loans		XY Cash available	Y 90-day loan due
Unplanned Loans		Y.....Cash available	Y Loan due
Sell Stock		X Negotiate..... Y (Receive funds)	
Buy Securities		X Y	
		Y	
Sell Securities		X.....Interest accrues.....Y (Cash available)	
Marketing			
Promotion	X	Y Greatest impact	
Marketing		XY Greatest impact	
Product Development	X		Y Greatest impact

Key: X = Decision
Y = Results

The Reports

The preceding sections describe the industry from an operational point of view. Now, for easy reference, part of the same information and some new information will be presented in outline form, parallel to the makeup of the accounting reports.

Exhibit I—Decision Form

The decisions each firm formulates will be submitted on a form identical to Exhibit I. The top line is for identification and complete information is essential to the administration of the simulation.

The succeeding title lines identify the information to be entered in the box directly below the title. Each line will be punched on a computer card. Card 1 contains financial decisions for the firm. Cards 2–4 are for Product 1 decisions; cards 5–7, for Product 2; and cards 8–10, for Product 3.

Card #1—Financial Decisions

Box 1—The number of $1,000 of plant and equipment purchase, e.g. $50,000 = 50.

Box 2—Securities purchase indicated by a plus (+), sale indicated by a minus (−).

Box 3—Dividends are paid in multiples of $1,000, e.g. $50,000 = 50.

Boxes 4–7—The number of $1,000 desired, e.g. $200,000 = 200. Loans are retired automatically.

Box 8—Forecast of Firm's Cash Position at end of quarter.

Cards #2, 5, and 8—Marketing Decisions

Box 1—Price of Product in dollars per unit, e.g. $7.70 = 7.70.

Box 2—The Marketing budget in thousands of dollars, e.g. $310,000 = 310.

Box 3—The Promotion budget in thousands of dollars, e.g. $31,500 = 31.5.

Box 4—The Product Development budget in thousands of dollars, e.g. $50,000 = 50.

Box 5—The Market Research budget in thousands of dollars, e.g. $82,000 = 82.

Box 6A—Price to be tested by Market Research in cents per unit, e.g. $18.00 = 1800.

6B—Marketing budget to be tested by Market Research in $1,000.

Box 7A—Quality of product = sum of fabrication and assembly labor budgets plus cost per unit of raw material and purchased parts. To be tested by Market Research, in cents per unit, e.g. $9.00 = 900.

7B—Product Development budget to be tested by Market Research in $1,000, e.g. $21,500 = 21.

Box 8—Forecast of number of items of product that will be sold during quarter.

Cards #3, 6, and 9—Fabrication Department Decisions

Box 1—Cost per unit of raw material to be purchased, e.g. $1.10 = 1.10.

Box 2—Scheduled production rate for the following period. This must be filled in to insure enough raw material for the first 4 weeks of next period.

Box 3—Scheduled production rate for present quarter, e.g. 265,000 units/quarter = 265.

Box 4—Labor is scheduled on a per unit basis, e.g. $1.00 = 1.00. The quality level will be met, reducing quantity if there are not enough productive hours available.

Box 5—The *total* number of men assigned to a department of a product. This *includes* men previously assigned *plus or minus* men hired or fired *plus* men transferred from another department and/or product.

Box 6—Number of new employees desired (+) or number of employees to be released (−) from the firm.

Box 7—Total number of overtime hours desired, e.g. 60,000 = 60,000.

Box 8—Forecast of number of items of product that will be produced during quarter.

Cards #4, 7, and 10—Assembly Department Decisions

Format identical to cards 3, 6, and 9 with Purchased Parts in place of Raw Materials.

Box 8—Forecast of product's Operating Profit for quarter.

Exhibit I

Management Simulation—Decision Form

Industry 21 Firm 1 Period 4 Can Group 5

Purchase Plant $1000	Purchase Securities $1000	Dividends $1000	90-Day Loans $1000	One-Year Loan $1000	Five-Year Notes $1000		Sell Stock $1000			Ending Cash Position
50.	0.	100.	0.	0.	0		0		1	
PRODUCT 1	//////////	//////////	//////////	//////////	//////////	//////////	//////////	//////////	//////////	//////////
Price of Product $ per unit	Marketing Budget $1000	Promotion Budget $1000	Prod. Dev. Budget $1000	Mkt. Res. Budget $1000	MR- Price CPU	MR- Mkt. $1000	MR- Qual. CPU	MR- P.D. $1000		Forecast Orders
7.70	430.	0.	50.	0.	0	0	0	0	2	
Raw Mat'l $ per unit	Fab. Production Rates Next Pd. 1000 units	This Pd. 1000 units	Fab. Labor $ per unit	Fab. # Men Assigned	# Men Hire (+) Fire (-)		Fab. Overtime # Hours			Finished Goods Production
1.10	240.	240.	1.00	260.	10		0		3	
Purchased Parts $ per unit	Asm. Production Rates Next Pd. 1000 units	This Pd. 1000 units	Asm. Labor $ per unit	Asm. # Men Assigned	# Men Hire (+) Fire (-)		Asm. Overtime # Hours			Product Profit (Loss)
.40	240.	240.	.70	182.	10		12000		4	

PRODUCT 2										
Price of Product $ per unit	Marketing Budget $1000	Promotion Budget $1000	Prod. Dev. Budget $1000	Mkt. Res. Budget $1000	MR- Price CPU	MR- Mkt. $1000	MR- Qual. CPU	MR- P.D. $1000		Forecast Orders
20.00	80.	0.	22.	65.	1200	0	900	0	5	
Raw Mat'l $ per unit	Fab. Production Rates Next Pd. 1000 units	This Pd. 1000 units	Fab. Labor $ per unit	Fab. # Men Assigned	# Men Hire (+) Fire (-)		Fab. Overtime # Hours			Finished Goods Production
2.20	40	40	2.40	106	0		0		6	
Purchased Parts $ per unit	Asm. Production Rates Next Pd. 1000 units	This Pd. 1000 units	Asm. Labor $ per unit	Asm. # Men Assigned	# Men Hire (+) Fire (-)		Asm. Overtime # Hours			Product Profit (Loss)
.65	40	40	4.50	200	0		0		7	
PRODUCT 3										
Price of Product $ per unit	Marketing Budget $1000	Promotion Budget $1000	Prod. Dev. Budget $1000	Mkt. Res. Budget $1000	MR- Price CPU	MR- Mkt. $1000	MR- Qual. CPU	MR- P.D. $1000		Forecast Orders
0.	0.	0.	0.	0.	0	0	0	0	8	
Raw Mat'l $ per unit	Fab. Production Rates Next Pd. 1000 units	This Pd. 1000 units	Fab. Labor $ per unit	Fab. # Men Assigned	# Men Hire (+) Fire (-)		Fab. Overtime # Hours			Finished Goods Production
0.	0.	0.	0.	0.	0		0		9	
Purchased Parts $ per unit	Asm. Production Rates Next Pd. 1000 units	This Pd. 1000 units	Asm. Labor $ per unit	Asm. # Men Assigned	# Men Hire (+) Fire (-)		Asm. Overtime # Hours			Product Profit (Loss)
0.	0.	0.	0.	0.	0		0		10	

Exhibit II

Income Statement

MANAGEMENT SIMULATION

INDUSTRY 21 FIRM 1

INCOME STATEMENT PERIOD 4

TOTAL SALES REVENUE		$ 2693691.
COST OF GOODS SOLD		
FABRICATION LABOR	343344.	
ASSEMBLY LABOR	333002.	
RAW MATERIALS	363220.	
PURCHASED PARTS	127151.	
OVERTIME PREMIUM	0.	1166717.
GROSS PROFIT		1526974.
FACTORY OVERHEAD		
INDIRECT LABOR	1674.	
SUPERVISION	138215.	
MAINTENANCE	68473.	
DEPRECIATION	50405.	258768.

SELLING AND ADMINISTRATIVE EXPENSES		
MARKETING	390000.	
PROMOTION	0.	
COMMISSIONS AND SALESMENS EXPENSE	184185.	
WAREHOUSE AND SHIPPING	42781.	
MARKET RESEARCH	65000.	
PRODUCT DEVELOPMENT	72000.	
ADMINISTRATIVE	70989.	824955.
OPERATING PROFIT		443251.
INTEREST EXPENSE		5625.
SECURITY INCOME		0.
TAXABLE INCOME		437626.
INCOME TAX		227566.
N E T I N C O M E		$ 210060.

P L A N T R E P O R T

PLANT CAPACITY, PERIOD 5	$ 2015815.
LOSS FROM DEPRECIATION	50395.
GAIN FROM NEW INVESTMENT	50000.
PLANT CAPACITY, PERIOD 6	$ 2015419.
TOTAL NUMBER OF EMPLOYEES	807.

B U S I N E S S I N D E X (SEASONALLY ADJUSTED)

PERIODS 1 TO 4 (ACTUAL)	685	671	657	629
PERIODS 5 TO 8 (ESTIMATED)	650	668	708	714
PERIODS 9 TO 12 (ESTIMATED)	756	725	737	719

Exhibit II—Income Statement

This report summarizes income figures, plant status and the business index.

INCOME STATEMENT

Down through OPERATING PROFIT, this simply totals the individual product reports.

INTEREST EXPENSE = FINANCIAL INTEREST

SECURITY INCOME is earned and entered at the rate of 1% per period, on the value of securities held throughout each period.

TAXABLE INCOME = OPERATING PROFIT + SECURITY INCOME − INTEREST EXPENSE

INCOME TAX = 52% of taxable income. There is an immediate tax rebate in case of loss up to the amount of taxes your firm has paid.

NET INCOME = TAXABLE INCOME − INCOME TAX

PLANT REPORT

This report summarizes the value of plant during the period following the "date" of the report. This you will want to use in determining the maximum total labor force for next period, i.e., one man per $2,500 plant. The total number of employees for this period is also shown. This should be the total of men assigned to each department plus idle men, if any.

GAIN FROM NEW INVESTMENT = Plant purchase decision last period, which will be paid for this period. The extra plant will be available next period.

BUSINESS INDEX

The values of the index are precise for present and past periods but this accuracy of the forecasted values decreases as they become longer range.

Exhibit III—Balance Sheet

BALANCE SHEET

CASH = former value of same item plus net cash inflow for the period (which of course represents a reduction when negative).

SECURITIES = former value of same item plus purchase (or minus sale) of securities during the period concerned.

ACCOUNTS RECEIVABLE = approximately 30% of sales of current period.

INVENTORIES = the sum of the inventory valuation for individual products.

CURRENT ASSETS = the sum of four items just listed.

PLANT AND EQUIPMENT, NET = the end-of-period value of plant minus depreciation. This is the value the maximum number of efficient employees is dependent upon for the next period.

TOTAL ASSETS = CURRENT ASSETS + PLANT AND EQUIPMENT, NET.

ACCOUNTS PAYABLE = about 30 days' worth of Raw Material and Purchased Parts purchases and one-third of the marketing budget.

NOTES PAYABLE = total of all loans and notes due within one year, including portion of five-year notes due within one year.

TAXES = amount of taxes owned. In case of a loss, there is an immediate rebate, if tax credits exist, which will show under the Cash Flow Receipts. In case of a profit the tax owed will appear here to be paid next period.

CURRENT LIABILITIES = the sum of three items just listed.

LONG-TERM DEBT = amount of five-year notes not due within one year.

COMMON STOCK = number of shares and total par value.

SURPLUS = retained earnings.

TOTAL LIABILITIES AND EQUITY = CURRENT LIABILITIES plus three items just listed.

FINANCIAL RATIOS

1. TOTAL LIABILITIES TO TOTAL ASSETS =

$$\frac{\text{CURRENT LIABILITIES} + \text{LONG-TERM DEBT}}{\text{TOTAL ASSETS}}$$

2. LONG-TERM DEBT TO TOTAL ASSETS – self-explanatory.
3. QUICK RATIO =

$$\frac{\text{CASH} + \text{SECURITIES} + \text{ACCOUNTS RECEIVABLE}}{\text{CURRENT LIABILITIES}}$$

Exhibit III

Balance Sheet

INDUSTRY 21 FIRM 1

BALANCE SHEET PERIOD 4

CASH		1252287.
SECURITIES		0.
ACCOUNTS RECEIVABLE		997663.
INVENTORIES		
RAW MATERIALS	131569.	
PURCHASED PARTS	79961.	
WORK IN PROCESS	390667.	
FABRICATED PARTS	92236.	
FINISHED GOODS	254397.	948830.
CURRENT ASSETS		3198780.
PLANT AND EQUIPMENT, NET		2015815.
TOTAL ASSETS		5214595.
ACCOUNTS PAYABLE		319444.
NOTES PAYABLE		500000.
TAXES		227566.
CURRENT LIABILITIES		1047010.
LONG TERM DEBT		0.
COMMON STOCK	500000. SHARES	2017500.
SURPLUS		2150084.
TOTAL LIABILITIES AND EQUITY		5214595.

TOTAL LIAB TO TOTAL ASSETS	LONG TERM DEBT TO TOTAL ASSETS	QUICK RATIO	CURRENT RATIO	FIXED CHARGES COVERAGE
20 0/0	0 0/0	2.15	3.06	97.99

STOCK PRICE $ 25 3/8

C A S H   F L O W

CASH SALES	1696028.
CASH FROM ACCOUNTS RECEIVABLE	1144264.
INCOME FROM SECURITIES	0.
CASH FROM SALE UF SECURITIES	0.
CASH FROM 90 DAY UNSECURED LOAN	0.
CASH FROM 90 DAY SECURED LOAN	0.
CASH FROM 90 DAY DISTRESS LOAN	0.
CASH FROM ONE YEAR LOAN	0.
CASH FROM FIVE YEAR NOTE	0.
CASH FROM SALE OF STOCK (0. SHARES)	0.
T O T A L R E C E I P T S	2840292.
TOTAL CASH EXPENSES (INCL INTEREST)	2267007.
TAXES PAID	398623.
SECURITIES PURCHASED	0.
CAPITAL EXPENDITURES, PLANT	50000.
DIVIDENDS PAID	50000.
REPAYMENT OF 90 DAY LOANS	0.
REPAYMENT OF ONE YEAR LOAN	0.
REPAYMENT OF FIVE YEAR NOTE	0.
T O T A L D I S B U R S E M E N T S	2765630.
N E T C A S H I N F L O W	74662.

4. $\text{CURRENT RATIO} = \dfrac{\text{CURRENT ASSETS}}{\text{CURRENT LIABILITIES}}$

5. FIXED CHARGES COVERAGE =

$$\frac{\text{Average * Profit Before Taxes + Depreciation}}{\dfrac{\text{Sinking Fund}}{(1 - \text{Tax Rate})} + \text{Interest}}$$

STOCK PRICE = dollars per share.

CASH FLOW

Most entries are self-explanatory except to note the following:

CASH FROM ACCOUNTS RECEIVABLE = opening accounts receivable, normally about 30% of sales of prior period.

INCOME FROM SECURITIES = 1% of value of securities held or sold this period.

CASH FROM SECURITIES, NOTES and STOCK appear only when applicable.

TOTAL CASH EXPENDITURES = SELLING AND ADMINISTRATIVE EXPENSES + INTEREST + SUPERVISION AND MAINTENANCE COSTS + \$900 × Total Number of Men + TOTAL COST OF OVERTIME + Opening Accounts Payable − Closing Accounts Payable + Raw Material and Purchased Parts Purchases.

REPAYMENT OF FIVE–YEAR NOTE − amount of 5-year note repaid during the period.

* This period and last 3 periods.

Exhibit IV—Product Statement

PRODUCT INCOME STATEMENT

REVENUE FROM SALES = price times sales volume for the product concerned.

COST OF GOODS SOLD AT STANDARD COSTS = the sum of the following five items.

FABRICATION LABOR
ASSEMBLY LABOR
RAW MATERIALS
PURCHASED PARTS

} = Standard unit cost if there have been no changes. Weighted average standard unit cost during periods when changes are being effected.

OVERTIME PREMIUM = Additional cost of overtime hours scheduled at \$1.80 per hour for fabrication department and \$1.20 per hour for assembly department.

GROSS PROFIT = REVENUE FROM SALES – COST OF GOODS SOLD AT STANDARD COST

FACTORY OVERHEAD

INDIRECT LABOR = \$900 × number of idle men + labor inefficiency costs.

SUPERVISION = about \$160 per worker.

MAINTENANCE – depends on total assembly department production volume, about \$200 per 1,000 units produced for low volumes, \$300 per 1,000 units for high volume production + side costs of increasing plant capacity.

DEPRECIATION = 2.5% of plant value allocated on the basis of direct labor hours.

SELLING AND ADMINISTRATIVE EXPENSE

MARKETING, PROMOTION, PRODUCT DEVELOPMENT AND MARKET RESEARCH = budgets.

COMMISSIONS AND SALESMEN'S EXPENSES = commission rate of 5% of sales dollars + about 15 cents per unit sold.

WAREHOUSE AND SHIPPING = three cents per unit of total work in process and fabricated parts inventories on hand plus three cents per unit of finished goods inventory plus one per cent of the finished goods inventory evaluation plus ten cents per unit sold plus one and a half per cent of the value of raw material and purchased parts inventories on hand.

ADMINISTRATIVE = one administrator for about every 50,000 units produced in each department (i.e., Product 1 Assembly, Product 1 Fabrication, etc.) at about \$16,000 per year. In cases of decreasing production, administrators are laid off at the rate of about 20% of the extra men being dismissed each period. PLUS one top executive for each million dollars worth of plant at an average salary of about \$25,000 per year allocated to products on the basis of direct labor hours plus costs associated with hiring and firing men and handling securities.

OPERATING PROFIT = GROSS PROFIT – FACTORY OVERHEAD – SELLING AND ADMINISTRATIVE EXPENSES

Exhibit IV

Product Statement

INDUSTRY 21 FIRM 1 PRODUCT 2

INCOME STATEMENT PERIOD 4

REVENUE FROM SALES, AT $ 20.00 PER UNIT		$ 657180.
COST OF GOODS SOLD AT STANDARD COST		
FABRICATION LABOR, AT $ 2.40 PER UNIT	78862.	
ASSEMBLY LABOR, AT $ 4.50 PER UNIT	147865.	
RAW MATERIALS, AT $ 2.20 PER UNIT	72290.	
PURCHASED PARTS, AT $ 0.65 PER UNIT	21358.	
OVERTIME PREMIUM	0.	320375.
GROSS PROFIT		336805.
FACTORY OVERHEAD		
INDIRECT LABOR	1166.	
SUPERVISION	52773.	
MAINTENANCE	8186.	
DEPRECIATION	19113.	81239.
SELLING AND ADMINISTRATIVE EXPENSES		
MARKETING	80000.	
PROMOTION	0.	
COMMISSIONS AND SALESMENS EXPENSE	38859.	
WAREHOUSE AND SHIPPING	7751.	
PRODUCT DEVELOPMENT	22000.	
MARKET RESEARCH	65000.	
ADMINISTRATIVE	10459.	224069.
OPERATING PROFIT		$ 31497.

PRODUCTION

	FABRICATION DEPT.	ASSEMBLY DEPT.
PRODUCTION VOLUME, UNITS	39744.	39744.
W.I.P. INVENTORY, UNITS	9936.	6624.
NUMBER OF MEN HIRED OR FIRED	0.	0.
NUMBER OF MEN BUDGETED	106.	200.
NUMBER OF MEN WORKING	106.	200.
NUMBER OF HOURS AVAILABLE	53000.	100000.
PERCENT HOURS UTILIZED	100.	99.
NUMBER OF HOURS OVERTIME	0.	0.

INVENTORIES

RAW MATERIALS AT $ 2.20 PER UNIT, 15296. UNITS
PURCHASED PARTS AT $ 0.65 PER UNIT, 32565. UNITS
FABRICATED PARTS AT $ 4.60 AVERAGE PER UNIT 3333. UNITS

FINISHED GOODS, IN UNITS		
BEGINNING		12106.
PRODUCTION		39744.
GOODS AVAILABLE		51850.
ORDERS RECEIVED	32859.	
SALES LOST	0.	
SALES VOLUME		32859.
ENDING, AT $ 9.75 AVERAGE COST PER UNIT		18991.
SHARE OF INDUSTRY UNIT SALES VOLUME, PERCENT		2.

RESEARCH REPORT	PRICE	QUALITY	PROD DEVEL	MARKETING	SALES UNITS
	18.00	9.00	0.	0.	42209.

PRODUCTION

This report covers both Fabrication and Assembly Departments separately.

PRODUCTION VOLUME, UNITS = number of units that are put into that department during period.

W.I.P. INVENTORY, UNITS = number of units in process at end of period, i.e., Fabrication Dept., 3 weeks' amount of production, Assembly Dept., 2 weeks' amount.

NUMBER OF HOURS AVAILABLE = 500 hours per man previously assigned and less for men transferred or hired plus NUMBER OF HOURS OVERTIME. (See Labor Force – Production.)

PERCENT HOURS UTILIZED – an indicator of the efficiency of labor force =

$$\frac{\text{number of hours needed to produce at desired production rate}}{\text{NUMBER OF HOURS AVAILABLE}}$$

INVENTORIES

FINISHED GOODS, PRODUCTION = number of units completed by Assembly Dept.

SHARE OF INDUSTRY SALES VOLUME, PERCENT = percent of units sold for all products.

MARKET RESEARCH

SALES = number of units.

Exhibit V—Industry Report

Each firm in an industry receives the identical Industry Report which presents gross statistics on all competitors in an industry. The data presented under the titles "Profit and Loss" and "Financial Condition" are expressed in $1,000 and are accurate. The data under "Individual Products" with the exception of "Price" are *not* accurate but have been randomized. This gives you an indication of what other firms are doing but prevents the immediate identifying of shifts in tactics. In most instances these figures are within 20 percent of their actual values.

Price and Direct CPU are in dollars; Marketing (which includes Promotion) and Product Development budgets are $1,000 and Sales Units are in 1,000s. Products 1, 2, and 3 are listed from left to right.

Appendix 1 — Determination of Production Output

Labor Efficiency Build-up

To enable accurate planning of production schedules, Exhibit VI is provided to show the rate of increase in the efficiency of new men. The chart shows the number of standard hours (to the nearest half-hour) of production available in any given week from one hired or transferred man. For example, one newly hired man will provide 4.0 standard production hours in the first week of the quarter and will gradually work up to full efficiency by the end of the quarter, or approximately 41½ hours a week (500 hours per quarter divided by 12).

Exhibit VI can be used to determine the maximum number of units that enter a department each week. To do this, the following steps must be taken:

(1) The number of men in each of the six labor categories indicated in Exhibit VI must be determined.

(2) The number of men in each category is then multiplied by the appropriate standard production hours figure from Exhibit VI. This will give the number of hours available in each category.

(3) The hours available from Step 2 can then be converted into a unit production rate by using the departmental labor cost per unit figure on the decision sheet and by recognizing that workers are being paid \$1.80 per hour. These numbers when added will indicate the amount of production in units that can enter a department each week.

These steps may be summarized by the following formula:

$$\begin{matrix}\text{Number of units} \\ \text{entering department}\end{matrix} = \frac{\$1.80}{\text{labor cost per unit}} \times \sum_{n=1}^{6} M_n \times H_{n,w}$$

M_n = Number of workers in category n

$H_{n,w}$ = Number of standard hours of production that a worker in category n can produce in week w

Exhibit VII shows a work sheet which has been filled out using the preceding three steps and the following data:

3 men have been hired

3 men have been transferred from another product in the same department

2 men have been transferred from another department in the same product

1 man has been transferred from another department and another product

Exhibit V

Industry Report

I N D U S T R Y 42   P E R I O D 6

I N D U S T R Y   R E P O R T

F I R M 1		STOCK PRICE	13 3/4	DIVIDENDS PAID	50000.		
PROFIT AND LOSS		FINANCIAL COND		INDIVIDUAL PRODUCTS			
SALES RVNUE	2892.	CASH	112.	PRICE	16.15	7.00	0.
TOT EXPENSE	2516.	INVENTORY	879.	MARKETING	152.28	356.92	0.
OPER PROFIT	376.	PLANT-EQUP	2196.	PROD DEVEL	26.42	99.35	0.
SECURTY INC	0.	TOT LIAB	987.	DIRECT CPU	8.96	2.93	0.
NET EARNED	175.	COM EQUITY	3183.	SLS UNITS	38.43	324.82	0.

F I R M 2		STOCK PRICE	11 1/2	DIVIDENDS PAID	0.		
PROFIT AND LOSS		FINANCIAL COND		INDIVIDUAL PRODUCTS			
SALES RVNUE	2091.	CASH	105.	PRICE	7.65	13.45	0.
TOT EXPENSE	1845.	INVENTORY	1519.	MARKETING	268.73	80.28	0.
OPER PROFIT	246.	PLANT-EQUP	1977.	PROD DEVEL	0.	0.	0.
SECURTY INC	0.	TOT LIAB	730.	DIRECT CPU	3.40	5.86	0.
NET EARNED	115.	COM EQUITY	3581.	SLS UNITS	225.47	35.52	0.

F I R M 3		STOCK PRICE	6 1/2	DIVIDENDS PAID	0.		
PROFIT AND LOSS		FINANCIAL COND		INDIVIDUAL PRODUCTS			
SALES RVNUE	3201.	CASH	616.	PRICE	7.50	10.50	0.
TOT EXPENSE	2631.	INVENTORY	787.	MARKETING	384.59	207.82	0.
OPER PROFIT	570.	PLANT-EQUP	2542.	PROD DEVEL	59.29	44.21	0.
SECURTY INC	0.	TOT LIAB	1850.	DIRECT CPU	3.12	5.01	0.
NET EARNED	265.	COM EQUITY	3183.	SLS UNITS	295.52	88.17	0.

```
F I R M   4        STOCK PRICE   5 3/4           DIVIDENDS PAID        0.
 PROFIT AND LOSS     FINANCIAL COND       INDIVIDUAL PRODUCTS
SALES RVNUE  2608.  CASH           828.  PRICE                8.10   14.00     0.
TOT EXPENSE  2229.  INVENTORY      750.  MARKETING          267.57  138.15     0.
OPER PROFIT   378.  PLANT-EQUP    2113.  PROD DEVEL          24.70   19.53     0.
SECURTY INC     0.  TOT LIAB      1473.  DIRECT CPU           4.09    6.69     0.
NET EARNED    174.  COM EQUITY    3104.  SLS UNITS          202.14   65.53     0.

F I K M   5        STOCK PRICE   5 7/8           DIVIDENDS PAID        0.
 PROFIT AND LOSS     FINANCIAL COND       INDIVIDUAL PRODUCTS
SALES RVNUE  2586.  CASH           117.  PRICE                7.50   13.00     0.
TOT EXPENSE  2340.  INVENTORY     1353.  MARKETING          288.57  185.24     0.
OPER PROFIT   246.  PLANT-EQUP    3310.  PROD DEVEL          65.68   44.09     0.
SECURTY INC     0.  TOT LIAB      2621.  DIRECT CPU           3.29    5.56     0.
NET EARNED     88.  COM EQUITY    3039.  SLS UNITS          255.94   59.80     0.
```

Exhibit VI

Standard Production Hours of Output Obtained from Each Man Each Week in a Quarter

Week	1	2	3	4	5	6	7	8	9	10	11	12
Newly hired men	4.0	7.5	11.0	14.5	18.0	21.0	24.5	28.0	31.5	35.0	38.0	41.5
Men transferred across products in same dept.	31.0	33.5	35.5	37.5	39.5	41.5	41.5	41.5	41.5	41.5	41.5	41.5
Men transferred across depts. in same product	25.0	27.5	30.0	32.0	34.5	37.0	39.0	41.5	41.5	41.5	41.5	41.5
Men transferred across both depts. and products	16.5	19.5	22.0	25.0	28.0	30.5	33.5	36.0	39.0	41.5	41.5	41.5
Idle men assigned to work	31.0	33.5	37.5	39.5	41.5	41.5	41.5	41.5	41.5	41.5	41.5	41.5
Experienced men	41.5	41.5	41.5	41.5	41.5	41.5	41.5	41.5	41.5	41.5	41.5	41.5

1 idle man has been put to work
22 men are experienced, having worked in this department and on this product last period
The labor cost per unit in this department is 90¢

For example, to find the maximum number of units, entering a department, that can be handled by newly hired workers in week 1, multiply number of men (3) times hours per man (4.0) times $1.80 and divide by the labor cost per unit ($.90). Thus three newly hired men will allow up to 24 units to be introduced during the first week of a quarter's production. Altogether the hired, transferred, and experienced men in this department will permit 2231 units to be introduced into the department during the first week. This work sheet can thus be used to determine the production rate which can be obtained each week from the work force in a department.

Production Processing Delays

A second factor to be considered in planning of finished goods production is the time delay associated with changing work-in-process inventory levels to support the new production rate. Exhibit VIII contains a sample problem to show how many units there are in each of the inventories each week. The following data was used for this problem.

Beginning raw materials inventory = 20 units
Beginning purchased parts inventory = 24 units
Beginning fabricated parts inventory = 0
Fabrication production rate = 5 units per week
Assembly production rate = 4 units per week
Raw materials ordered at beginning of period = 60 units
Purchased parts ordered at beginning of period = 48 units

Changes in Production Rates

Changes in production rates from one period to another result in moderate administrative costs. In addition, increases in production rates take time to take effect. Exhibit IX shows the relationship between the size of the production increase and the time required to implement this increase. The previous period's weekly production rate is the number of units that entered a department in the final week. Decreases in production rate take place immediately.

For example, any increase greater than 20% but less than or equal to 25% will take four weeks to accomplish. During these four weeks,

Exhibit VII

Work Sheet for Product X, Dept. Y

(all values in units)

1. Week	1	2	3	4	5	6	7	8	9	10	11	12
2. Hired	24	45	66	87	108	126	147	168	189	210	228	249
3. Diff. products	186	201	213	225	237	249	249	249	249	249	249	249
4. Diff. depts.	100	110	120	128	138	148	156	166	166	166	166	166
5. Across both	33	39	44	50	56	61	67	72	78	83	83	83
6. Idle men	62	67	75	79	83	83	83	83	83	83	83	83
7. Experienced men	1826	1826	1826	1826	1826	1826	1826	1826	1826	1826	1826	1826

8. Weekly prod. rate (add lines 2 through 7)	2231	2288	2344	2395	2448	2493	2528	2564	2591	2617	2635	2656
9. Amount of desired rate increase that can be implemented each week												
10. Total possible prod. rate (line 9 + previous period's weekly rate)												
11. Actual prod. rate per week (line 8 or 10, whichever is less).												

Exhibit VIII

Production Delays and Inventories

	raw materials inventory	1st week fab.	2nd week fab.	3rd week fab.	fabricated parts inventory	purchased parts inventory	1st week assemb.	2nd week assemb.	finished goods inventory
Week 1	20 - 15*	5				24 - 24			
Week 2	15 - 10	5	5			24 - 24			
Week 3	10 - 5	5	5	5		24 - 24			
Week 4	5 - 0	5	5	5	5 - 1	24 - 20	4		
Week 5	60 - 55	5	5	5	6 - 2	20 - 16	4	4	0 - 4
Week 6	55 - 50	5	5	5	7 - 3	16 - 12	4	4	0 - 8
Week 7	50 - 45	5	5	5	8 - 4	60 - 56	4	4	8 - 12
Week 8	45 - 40	5	5	5	9 - 5	56 - 52	4	4	12 - 16

Week 9	40 - 35	5	5	5	10 - 6	52 - 48	4	4	16 - 20
Week 10	35 - 30	5	5	5	11 - 7	48 - 44	4	4	20 - 24
Week 11	30 - 25	5	5	5	12 - 8	44 - 40	4	4	24 - 28
Week 12	25 - 20	5	5	5	13 - 9	40 - 36	4	4	28 - 32

* All inventories are "beginning of week—end of week"; that is, in the raw materials inventory, there are 20 units at the beginning of week 1 and 15 units at the end of week 1.

there will be a linear increase in production rate until the desired rate is reached.

There is only one exception to this rule. There is a one-week lag in starting production on a new product; thereafter if sufficient raw materials and workers are available, production is taken into the fabrication department at the scheduled rate. The assembly production rate will depend on the fabricated parts and purchased parts inventories.

Predicting Actual Production Rate

If the production rate increase is being provided by newly hired or transferred men, prediction of the actual production rate becomes more complex. There must be sufficient raw materials, fabricated parts, and purchased parts available. There must be enough plant and equipment for the number of men assigned. If these inventories and facilities are available, the production rate actually achieved in any one week will be limited either by the rate at which the desired increase in production can be implemented or by the inefficiency of the new men.

The following example illustrates how these two factors determine production rate. Assume that in this department the production rate achieved in the final week of the preceding period was 1800 units and the desired production rate is 2700 units per week. Since a 50% increase is desired, 9 weeks will be required to achieve this increase; in other words, the maximum increase that can be implemented is 100 units more each week (900 units increase ÷ 9 weeks required for the increase). The work sheet in Exhibit X can be expanded.

In this example, note that production rate is limited in the first seven weeks by the time required to implement a 50% increase in production; in the last five weeks, production rate is limited by the inefficiency of the new men. The desired rate of 2,700 units per week will not be achieved in this period.

Using this work sheet will enable you to predict accurately the rate at which goods will enter a department each week in the decision period. It will also enable you to calculate the amount of production you will achieve; adding up the production for all 12 weeks will equal Production Volume on the Quarterly Report.

Exhibit IX

Relationship Between Size of Production Increase and Time to Implement Increase

Increase of desired weekly prod. rate over previous period's final weekly production rate	≤ 10%	15%	20%	25%	30%	35%	40%	45%	50%	55%	60%	more than 60%
No. of weeks required to implement the desired increase	1	2	3	4	5	6	7	8	9	10	11	12

Exhibit X

Work Sheet (continued from Exhibit VII)

Week	1	2	3	4	5	6	7	8	9	10	11	12
8. Weekly prod. rate (add lines 2 through 7)	2231	2288	2344	2395	2448	2493	2528	2564	2591	2617	2635	2656
9. Amount of desired rate increase that can be implemented each week	100	200	300	400	500	600	700	800	900	900	900	900
10. Total possible prod. rate (line 9 + previous period's weekly rate)	1900	2000	2100	2200	2300	2400	2500	2600	2700	2700	2700	2700
11. Actual prod. rate per week (line 8 or 10, whichever is less).	1900	2000	2100	2200	2300	2400	2500	2564	2591	2617	2635	2656

In this example, note that production rate is limited

Appendix B

Management Control Methods—The Cash Forecast

Purposes: Profitable firms are not always solvent ones. A company is interested not only in maintaining an excess of revenues over costs, but in maintaining a balance of cash and short-term securities large enough to finance their operations. Cash management is especially a problem in firms which are growing and in firms where for one reason or another normal inflows of cash through accounts receivable or other sources have been slowed down or cut off.

The problem is illustrated in the Management Simulation. You are involved with what will become very profitable ventures. Yet sizable investments for research, for plant, for building and training an employee staff, for initial production, for distribution and marketing efforts, etc., must be paid out in cash *before any sales revenue is received in cash*. Most of the major cash expenses to support new investments in facilities or to support the added wage costs, sales costs, etc., associated with a growth in share of market must be met before the cash income is received. Failure to anticipate the cash needs of an expanding business and to plan so that these needs will be met at a reasonable financing cost is one of the major causes for the decline and fall of business organizations.

How to Make a Forecast: Making a cash forecast is tedious, but not really very difficult. It involves being willing to make some SWAG estimates on what sales will be or on what some expenses will amount to, but it does not involve complicated arithmetic. Like all forecasts, a cash forecast will be subject to error. To minimize the danger of taking your forecast too seriously, it should be at least checked—and perhaps remade from scratch—regularly and often. If crucial figures (like sales revenue) are hard to pin down, you may want to make as many as three separate forecasts:

1. An expected forecast: using what you think are the most likely values for all inflows or outflows.
2. A conservative forecast: adjusting your estimates so that you make expense items higher than you reasonably expect them to be and income items lower than you expect them to be.
3. An optimistic forecast: adjusting your expenses down and your income items up, within reason.

Unless you know you will have enough cash and really want only to find out what you will have available to invest in new opportunities, #1 and #2 are more pertinent than #3.

Here is a format for a cash forecast that you might use in the simulation exercise. You should fill this out for at least two periods into the future, and ideally, for 4–8 periods into the future.

Cash balance at the beginning of the quarter	______
Add: cash receipts from	
Sales (⅔ of the sales for the quarter)	______
Collection of accounts receivable (the balance sheet amount, or ⅓ of sales from previous quarter)	______
Interest on securities (1% of face amount per quarter)	______
Sales of securities	______
Income tax refunds (only if you have lost or expect to lose money and have paid taxes against which your losses can be credited)	______
Cash Available: Total Receipts + Opening Balance	______
Subtract: cash disbursements for	
Payment of supplier accounts (⅔ of raw materials and purchased parts bought this quarter; remaining ⅓ of materials and parts bought preceding quarter)	______
Repayment of loans (check to make sure when your loans come due)	______
Dividend payments	______

Labor costs: hiring ($200/man) or firing ($50/man) ______

Wages (number of men, × $900) ______

Overtime ($3 × # hours, assembly; $3.60 × # hours, fabrication) ______

Supervision: $160 × number of workers ______

Indirect labor ($900 × number of idle men × labor efficiency factor) ______

Maintenance: $300 per 1,000 units produced ______

Investment in new plant (paid 1 quarter after it is ordered) – amount of investment + an extra 10–25% assessment of "side costs" ______

Administrative expenses: $4,000 per 50,000 units made + 25,000 per $1 million of plant ______

Marketing Costs:

Marketing (⅔ of this quarter's cost; ⅓ of previous quarter's cost) ______

Promotion ______

Product Development ______

Market Research ______

Commissions (5% of $ sales + $.15 × # of units sold) ______

Warehousing and shipping ($.04 × # of units in each inventory + 2% of $ value of raw material and purchased parts inventory) ______

Taxes (52% of expected profits) ______

Total Cash Disbursements ______

Cash balance or deficiency at end of quarter before bank loans or sales of stock ______

Additional financing to be sought (90-day notes, 1-year loans, 5-year notes, sale of stock)
(Stock sales result in cash inflow one quarter after they are requested) ______

Cash balance, beginning of next quarter ______

General Advice: Most effort should go into:

1. Making a good estimate of sales, and thus of sales revenue.
2. Recognizing when new hires, new plant, worker transfers, etc., will cut productive efficiency and raise unit labor costs.
3. Recognizing when payments for plant investment or repayment of loans come due.
4. Getting enough cash on hand by taking loans, etc., to insure that you will have some reserve against unforeseen expenses in each quarter.

Bibliography

Bachman, W. A., "Sun Oil Establishes a Management School," *The Oil and Gas Journal* (March 22, 1965).

Baff, E. M., M. A. Leslie, M. P. Van Slyke, "The Potential of Business Gaming Methods in Research," *Journal of Business* (October 1966).

Base, B. M., "Business Gaming for Organizational Research," *Management Science* (April 1964).

Bellman, R., C. E. Clark, D. G. Malcom, C. J. Craft, F. M. Ricciardi, "On the Construction of a Multi-Stage Multi-Person Business Game," *Operations Research* (August 1957).

Cohen, K. J., W. R. Dill, A. Kuehn, P. Winters, *The Carnegie Tech Management Game: An Experiment in Business Education* (Homewood, Ill.: Richard D. Irwin, 1964).

Cohen, K. J. and **E. Rhenman,** "The Role of Management Games in Education and Research," *Management Science* (January 1961).

Collins, B. E. and **H. Guetzkow,** *A Social Psychology of Group Process for Decision Making* (New York: John Wiley & Sons, 1964).

Cyert, R. M. and **J. G. March,** *A Behavioral Theory of the Firm* (Englewood Cliffs, N. J.: Prentice-Hall, 1963).

Dale, A. G. and **C. R. Klasson,** "Business Gaming," *Survey of American Collegiate Schools of Business* (Austin: Bureau of Business Research, The University of Texas, 1964).

Dill, W. R. and **Neil Doppelt,** "The Acquisition of Experience in a Complex Management Game," *Management Science* (October 1963).

Dill, W. R., J. R. Jackson, J. Sweeney (Editors), *Proceedings of the Conference on Business Games as Teaching Devices* (New Orleans: Tulane University, 1961).

Greenlaw, Paul S., L. W. Herron, R. H. Rawdon, *Business Simulation in Industrial and University Education* (Englewood Cliffs, N. J.: Prentice-Hall, 1962).

Henshaw, R. C. and **J. R. Jackson,** *The Executive Game* (Homewood, Ill.: Richard D. Irwin, 1966).

Hoffman, Rudolph, "War Games," Department of the Army, Office of the Chief of Military History, Washington 25, D. C., MS Number P–094, 1952.

Hoffman, T. R., "Programmed Heuristics and the Concept of Par in Business Games," *Behavioral Science* (April 1965).

Holt, C., J. Muth, F. Modigliani, H. Simon, *Planning Production, Inventories, and Work Force* (Englewood Cliffs, N. J.: Prentice-Hall, Inc., 1960).

Jackson, J. R., "Learning from Experience in Business Games," *California Management Review* (Winter 1959).

Learned, E. P., C. R. Christensen, K. R. Andrews, *Problems of General Management* (Homewood, Ill.: Richard D. Irwin, 1961).

Learned, E. P., C. R. Christensen, K. R. Andrews, W. D. Guth, *Business Policy, Text and Cases* (Homewood, Ill.: Richard D. Irwin, 1965).

McClelland, D. C., "Achievement Motivation Can Be Developed," *Harvard Business Review* (November-December 1965).

McClelland, D. C., *The Achieving Society* (Princeton: Van Nostrand, 1961).

McDonald, J. and **F. M. Ricciardi,** "The Business Decision Game," *Fortune* (March 1958).

McKenney, J. L., "An Evaluation of a Business Game in an MBA Curriculum," *Journal of Business* (July 1962).

McKenney, J. L., "An Evaluation of a Decision Simulation as a Learning Environment," *Management Technology* (May 1963).

Murray, H. J. R., *A History of Board Games* (London: Oxford University Press, 1952).

Proceedings of the National Symposium on Management Games (Lawrence: The University of Kansas, 1959).

Rosenbloom, R. S., "A Progress Report on a Study of First-Year Grades for the Experimental Section." (Unpublished Report, Harvard Business School, March 4, 1961.)

Sayre, Farrand, *Map Maneuvers,* Revised Edition (Springfield, Mass.: Springfield Printing and Binding Company, 1908).

Schrieber, A. N., "Gaming a New Way to Teach Business Decision Making," *University of Washington Business Review* (April 1958).

Shubik, M., "A Business Game for Teaching & Research Purposes," IBM RC–731 (Yorktown Heights, N. Y., 1963).

Shubik, M., "Gaming, Costs and Facilities." (Unpublished Report, Yale University, March 1964.)

Symonds, G. H., "A Study of Management Behavior by Use of Competitive Business Games," *Management Science* (September 1964).

Thomas, G. J., "The Genesis and Practice of Operational Gaming," *Proceedings of the First International Conference on Operational Research* (Baltimore: J. Wright Bristol, 1957).

Thorelli, H. B. and **R. L. Graves,** *International Operations Simulation* (New York: The Free Press, 1964).

von Neumann, J. and **O. Morgenstern,** *Theory of Games and Economic Behavior* (Princeton: Princeton University Press, 1947).

Weiner, M. G., *An Introduction to War Games,* P–1773 (Santa Monica: The RAND Corporation, August 1959).

Young, J. P., *A Survey of Historical Developments in War Games* (Baltimore: Operations Research Office, Johns Hopkins University, 1960).